A Journey Home

H. W. Warren

CIRCLE OF PENS
PUBLICATIONS

www.circleofpens.com

First Edition 2007 by
CIRCLE OF PENS PUBLICATIONS
www.circleofpens.com

ISBN 978-0-9552471-2-5
0-9552471-2-8

Cover and typeset by
Circle of Pens Publications & Erik L. Lloyd

Printed and bound in Great Britain by Cromwell Press, Trowbridge, Wiltshire

Acknowledgements

It is thanks to the impetus from Bill's sister Nancy Warren, now known as Pat Glasper, that this book was finally published.

Bill's children eagerly backed this push and through their collective effort his Canadian recollections can now come to light.

It is the author's family fond wish that there may be some friends of Bill Warren still left alive and mentioned in this book that they get to read of the author's experiences in which they played a part.

Thanks to Vivian Waters and Eric Warren for their contribution in the writing of Bill's biography; and thanks to Erik Lloyd and Peter Georgiadis for the design of the book's jacket.

Foreword

This autobiographical story is as factually correct as is possible, after a period of fifty years.

It is the story of a young immigrant to Canada in the nineteen thirties, and of his journey home after nearly five years, his adventures, riding the freight trains and hitch hiking across Canada in mid-winter. And subsequent Atlantic liner voyage home.

A series of flashbacks portrays his life on the prairies during the great depression of the thirties, and describes the drought and dust storms of that decade.

All characters actually existed, though some names are fictitious. All events actually happened, though once again certain small place names are doubtful.

The Wheale family
The Barton family
The Bruce family
The Surtees family

...are all true names and existed at that time.

H.W.Warren returned to Saskatchewan after fifty years and re-established an acquaintance with the Wheale family. Len Wheale, who was eight years old when he worked for his father, 'Sam', was still living at the same farm, though his son was now running it. And Mary Wheale, twelve years old at that time, now married and living in the same small town of Lipton. He also visited the Bruce farm and made contact with Stuart's widow.

I ~ Mountain Time

"Where'y' heading, buddy?"

The words hit me cold! I was standing by a row of empty box-cars in the vast marshalling yards of Winnipeg. Alone as I thought, in a reverie. Casually watching the Eastern Freight shunting fussily back and forth, preparing for its fifteen hundred mile journey, and I had every intention of being aboard when it pulled out.

The only answer was a bold one.

"London, England on that freight", I replied.

The two mounties, looking like giants in their greatcoats, fur hats and belted holsters, the stocks of their handguns very visible, had been running a flashlight up and down me and immediately answered in disbelief.

"You mean London, Ontario."

"No", I said, "London, England", adding "I have money awaiting me in Montreal for my passage home."

There was a long silence as they surveyed me. So much depended on their response.

It was a bright and starlit night. Still and icy cold with packed snow underfoot. I had already travelled a thousand miles, but there was much more than a thousand miles yet to go to reach Montreal, and then home to England.

***

It all began in early December 1934. I was working in a furniture repair shop, when out of the blue a twenty pound money order, "one hundred dollars!", arrived with a brief letter from my father: "Like to see you home for Christmas." Suddenly it was possible, difficult but possible.

After five years of depression, drought and wandering, the prospect of sooty old London appeared very attractive. But! One hundred dollars - more than I'd ever had in my life - would only pay for the ocean fare, and I was in Calgary, two thousand miles from the ocean. The Atlantic Ocean, where I would hope to board a transatlantic liner for England.

Like many people whose lives were restricted and lived in one small country, my Dad's knowledge of geography and particularly of distance was limited to say the least. He had enquired (as I found out later), found the trans-ocean fare from Canada to England was eighteen pounds, and sent me twenty. Having not the vaguest idea that I was almost as far from Montreal as he was!

However, I'd had considerable experience over the previous five years of "Riding the rods", i.e. travelling the freights, and hitch-hiking. But not in winter time.

It was already cold, the temperature hovering around zero Fahrenheit. The central Canadian winter is ruthless and unforgiving, one treats it as an enemy but never underestimates that enemy's power. It will strike at the least careless action, and when it has you down will not relent willingly. 'Frost' would be my insidious and daunting foe until I reached the east coast.

But the die was cast. A hundred dollars would burn in my pocket for months if I didn't use it for the purpose it was intended. And already my feet were itching.

I had an opportunity, a challenge. Now I needed a large helping of luck! But I was elated.

I was going home.

The very next day I made a wooden crate for my precious guitar, packed my old suitcase with all my worldly possessions and conveyed them to the Canadian Pacific freight office. I despatched them to be collected from the C.P. office in Montreal, and so finally burnt my bridges.

No second thoughts now.

The beginning of the journey

A cold sunny morning, a snow covered landscape but windless. Good! I was dressed for the Arctic. Felt boots and overshoes, two pairs of socks, long johns, trousers and denims, shirt, pullover, denim jacket and greatcoat. Cap with earflaps and fur lined leather mittens. Gloves would have been useless, though the mitts might be clumsy at times. I also carried a rolled blanket suspended at my back by a piece of string. My hands had to be free.

In my pocket was a razor and toothbrush, the one hundred dollar roll of notes which I had no intention of touching during the journey, and five or six dollars I already had from my last wages. This would, I hoped, sustain me across Canada.

I was warm, and had no intention of worrying about all the possible snags. I'd always had this urge to travel and once again was "on my way". I knew the railway yards at Calgary, and the previous day had made discreet enquiries of various rail workers. There were always rail men around, especially in the bigger yards, and they were generally quite helpful. Times were hard and they were well aware of how lucky they were to have secure jobs, and very conscious of the transients who travelled the railroads in a seemingly aimless searching for work.

It was the "cops" we had to look out for. The mounties were considered decent guys, but the railroad police had a very bad reputation. One did not tangle with them. One ran!

By mid morning I was idling the time away beside a shed on the tracks east of the city when shortly the double hoot in the distance signalled the approach of a train. As the locomotive passed me at a walking pace I walked beside it, then began trotting, not wanting to swing aboard until I had found an empty car. Sure enough, well before the train's end, an open door appeared. I jumped up. And now I had a big empty room for myself, hopefully for hundreds of miles. After a few minutes I shivered as I thought, 'I must now have done the first mile of my six thousand mile journey', and it was obvious that mine would be a lonely ride.

In summer there would have been many hobos aboard, but this was winter and they had all disappeared to the cities, east or west, lumber camps or Government Hostels that had been set up for the unemployed in all cities, since the beginning of the depression. At least the police shouldn't be worrying about searching for them, so my ride might be easier.

I settled in a corner and dozed the hours away as the train rolled through the bleak snow covered prairie. The action of the wheels, the rhythm, is slightly hypnotic, but after a few hours the momentum began to change. I was aroused from my dozing, opened the door and saw we were approaching a large town. The people of Medicine Hat call it a city, but in England it would be a small town, and regardless of its Indian and exotic sounding name it was laid on a regular grid iron pattern like all modern North American towns, and had little to distinguish it except one curiosity. Natural gas had been discovered a few years previously and the street lights were never extinguished. They glowed night and day.

But I had a personal memory, of one day a year previously, a recollection of riding an identical freight train, though with many other travellers on its top, sunning ourselves in the fall sun. We drew slowly into Medicine Hat and stopped. A farmer walked briskly towards the train.

"Any of you guys want work?" he asked.

"How much, what doing?" was the chorus in reply.

"A dollar a day pulling onions" was his response. Four of us jumped down, and after a few moments' discussion we piled into his old jalopy for the twenty mile drive to his farm which lay in an elbow of the South

Saskatchewan river. I had never seen a large river of the prairies before; it seemed so incongruous as it was so wide and deep, yet sullen, coming from nowhere and seemingly going nowhere, in a flat featureless landscape. The farmer fed us, showed us our bunks in the bunkhouse, and early next morning after a huge breakfast we were taken out to the fields.

Onions as far as the eye could see…

We had to pull them up, break the stalks and put them back down in rows to dry. Food was brought out to us at midday, then on again. The farmer had already hired four Chinamen who set the pace. We never did catch up with them. Pride made us try and emulate them but they had a looseness, an ease of movement we could not equal. And as the sun set early in late September, we straightened up, relieved the day was over, hungry and exhausted. We slept that night like the dead. But when we awoke there was a subtle difference. We looked uneasily at one another, suddenly realising it was too quiet, almost an uncanny silence. When we looked out of the window the explanation was there, a foot of snow muffling all sound and radically changing our prospects. Snow could come early, and at this time of the year it might thaw or it might freeze. Either way the onion crop would most likely rot, so with the capriciousness of the Canadian climate a food crop could turn into a dead loss overnight. The farmer appeared shortly, subdued and despondent; handing us a dollar each he merely said, "My crop's gone, sorry, boys. I'll run you into town after breakfast."

Now, once again I was entering Medicine Hat. It was late afternoon and almost dark. I knew from past experience it was best to leave a train before it stopped. If the railway cops were around they would be wandering its length whilst it was idle at the water tank. When it had slowed sufficiently I jumped, left the tracks and walked along a nearby road towards the lights. There I found Main Street and also a general store where I bought a loaf of bread for ten cents and two apples for five cents. I intended to survive on bread for the seven days I reckoned it would take to reach Montreal. I was hungry, and the bread tasted good as I walked slowly to the east side of town, and waited by a workman's shed just back about half a mile from where I could hear the train hissing gently at the water tank. Shortly afterwards with the long drawn-out double wail of its hooter, it was coming towards me. The minute the powerful headlights of the engine passed me I was running alongside, pacing myself to the speed of the train, and trying to judge where my empty box car was. Suddenly here it was, I grabbed the open door and jumped. So! There I was, back in my empty room again, a little puffed but feeling quite pleased with myself as luck had not deserted me yet. Nearly two hundred miles behind me now, but a sobering thought. A long cold night ahead through the empty badlands of Southern Alberta and into Saskatchewan. Hundreds of miles before we were likely to stop again, not that it mattered, as when I slid the door open all I could see was the bleak, flat, snow covered landscape. So with a shiver I closed the door, unrolled my blanket and curled up in a corner. Drowsing the time away to the steady rhythm of the wheels and thinking of a few months previously, of when in daylight I had been travelling this same route in a flat car, full of old iron, and four of us trying to find comfortable positions in it. When apparently from nowhere, galloping alongside trying to race the train, small delicate dog-sized animals. "Antelopes", somebody volunteered; he was probably right. Ten or a dozen, a small graceful herd lightly racing alongside, over a stone-encrusted flat scrubland. Truly the badlands lived up to their name, brown tufty grass, dry and arid. All of a sudden they veered off, away from the train, stopped equally unexpectedly, and stood with sheep-like stupidity watching the train as it passed. How they existed in such an inhospitable terrain was unimaginable, but they did bring life to this barren land.

As also did the ubiquitous gophers. Those squirrel-like creatures, the pests of the prairies. Living in underground colonies or towns, standing upright on their hind legs and tweeting at the first sign of trouble; racing down their burrows but quickly reappearing out of sheer curiosity. As prolific as rabbits and destroying acres of a farmer's grain. But they did have the sense to hibernate in winter, I thought as I struggled to keep warm. Now my favourite hill billy song, "The wreck of the Number Nine", was somehow intruding into my reverie with its

"T'was a cold winter night
not a star was in sight,
As the north wind came howling down the line."

I was becoming increasingly aware and alarmed at the cold temperature, which was obviously dropping dramatically. There was no wind, but still nights are often the coldest. And now as I began to shiver I jumped up and beat my arms against my body, jumping up and down, pacing back and forth the length of the boxcar; then once again when I felt sufficiently warmed I would lie down, but not to sleep. Alternately throughout the night I was up and down, keeping the circulation going, making sure my extremities kept warm. Knowing full well that to drop off to sleep in about minus twenty degrees Fahrenheit, fifty degrees of frost, could prove fatal.

A long, long night. I grew tired and kept peering out of the door for the first signs of daylight. In the early hours there was a change as the wheels clattered over many points, and looking out I saw the name "Swift Current" as we passed through this sleeping town. We were now into Saskatchewan and must be halfway through the night. Everybody else could sleep, but I dare not. Then imperceptibly the sky lightened in the east, and as daylight spread my fatigue fell away. We were travelling through the real fertile prairie now, farm houses appeared every once in a while. The sun rose over the flat plain as the buildings of the town of Moose Jaw became visible on the horizon.

Another large town (the inhabitants called it a city), another Indian name, supposedly derived from the creek it is situated on. Which itself the Indians said, was shaped like the jaw bone of a moose.

As the train slowed once again with the wheels stuttering over the points on the outskirts, I awaited my opportunity then jumped, and followed a side road into town, through to Main Street where I purchased another loaf

7

of bread. I had eaten the other one through the night. Within half an hour I was waiting within sight of the tracks on the east side of town, out of full sight until the train passed, and then running alongside, faster now as this time the train had a good start. I managed to grab a stanchion between two cars, and swung myself up and onto the ledge between the couplings, then I climbed the iron railings to get on top. But having gained the roof, the wind created by the speed of the train hit me, and I knew it would be very unwise to attempt to walk along the boardwalk on top, in search of my empty car. So I climbed down again and resigned myself to jigging about where I was, knowing that Regina was only sixty miles further on; the sun was shining, and here I was protected from the wind. We were passing through the huge flat plains, the wheatlands of Canada. Spacious farms and barns, at present deep in snow, and suffering terrible droughts in the summer. There was an air of stability and permanence, quite belied by the knowledge that only sixty years before, it was virgin untouched land, known only to the Indians and buffalo. And Regina, the city we were nearing had more reasons to call itself a city, as it was the provincial capital of Saskatchewan with its impressive parliament buildings, its university and even street cars. But it was less than a hundred years old and sited on a spot called "Pile of Bones". This in itself typified what had happened in the area in a few short years.

The roaming buffaloes, in an incredibly brief time, had been slaughtered for their hides; their bones littered the plains for many years, then, almost quickly, the bones had a value and were collected and transported to the east to be ground down for fertiliser.

So Regina was created on a "Pile of Bones" that no longer existed and named after the Queen.

The next two hours passed uneventfully; the view did not change. I moved about as much as was possible to keep warm, and was eventually relieved to see large buildings appearing in the distance.

I knew the city and its reputation amongst (illegal) travellers, for the thoroughness of its railway police, hence I also knew that I had to leave the train well before we entered the marshalling yards.

The train was still going too fast but I could wait no longer, and watching for a clear flat sloping area beside the track I quickly jumped, then rolled down the slight embankment. No harm done! I was unhurt and could now walk towards the centre feeling jubilant. Five hundred miles behind me in one day, I really was "on my way".

I had arrived in Regina as a British Boy immigrant nearly five years previously. And as an immigrant had only an immigration identification card in my possession. To leave Canada I had to have a Canadian passport, the application forms for which I would have to obtain from an official in Regina, have it filled in and officially stamped, then when I arrived in Ottawa, present it and claim a passport. It was just after noon when I located the correct office, and explained my purpose to the particular official who questioned me. He was extremely helpful, filled in the necessary form, explained where the passport office was in Ottawa, wishing me luck and a good crossing, and adding a rider, "Keep warm". Maybe he guessed my mode of transport, by the amount of clothing I was wearing!

I was hungry, as all the bread had gone before I left the train. So now to look up an old friend, Karl Springer.

Karl was an Austrian and a cabinet maker, and I had walked into a small workshop one winter day - my first winter in Canada, looking for work. Karl had directed me to the small office where presided the Governor.

Old Mr. Surtees the owner - I thought of him as old, he was probably fifty - was a small asthmatic Yorkshire man with a voice like flint, but a soft heart. He had emigrated from Yorkshire after the first World War, and now his accent was pure Canadian, but when he heard somebody with an English voice, especially my cockney harshness, it struck a chord he could not resist. So from the first he had treated me with almost paternal affection. He always wanted me to "say something", as if my voice conjured up something in his past, or a subconscious homesickness.

I had explained how I had worked in a piano factory in the "Old

Country" for two years, learning the trade of French polishing. He showed interest, and then proceeded to tell me how hard times were, before offering me a job at a dollar a day, with a snappy take it or leave it attitude, and adding "You can bunk down in Karl's room."

I accepted with alacrity.

He then added, apparently as an afterthought, "I suppose you're hungry." This I did not deny. "Ok", he said, "Get in the car and we will go and meet the folks."

Without more ado we climbed in, and he drove to his home on the south side of the city, where I was introduced to his wife and three teenage children. I then enjoyed a sumptuous meal, which I had difficulty in eating slowly, as I had not eaten all day. Mrs.Surtees was also small, but retiring, quite the opposite to her husband who talked incessantly. The two daughters, very Canadian and sophisticated were also intrigued by my cockney accent. They were eighteen and nineteen and I flowered with their attention. The son, Peter, was fifteen, and at that time said little, though later we got on very well together. It was an extremely pleasant evening, and later Mr.Surtees drove me back to his workshop, where once again I met Karl, who became a good friend and with whom I spent that first winter.

It was a frugal existence. A dollar a day one could just about live on. The room upstairs was comfortable, with two bunks, an oil cooking stove, table and chairs, and the main asset… central heating… with the usual huge furnace in the basement. Times were extremely hard that winter, and The Great Depression was evident everywhere. Unemployment, hobos, and no money was the norm.

Would that workshop on South Railway Street be the same? I was eighteen when I worked there, nearly three years before. A long gap, but conditions generally had altered very little in the intervening years. I refused to consider the possibility of change, as I strode determinedly towards my destination.

And my luck held!

There was the little boss in his little office, there was Karl working away, unchanging. And there was also old George Duetsch the upholsterer. Incredible… it seemed like yesterday, it was unbelievable.

The boss came out of his office, "Well, well, well!" he said, in his sharp flinty voice, "look who's here, I bet he wants his job back."

"Hi Guv, hi you guys", I said, "but no thanks, I'm on my way home."

"What do you mean?" he asked in disbelief.

"London, England, Home", I replied. For once, words failed this articulate little man, and when I had explained my intentions, amid many interruptions, he found his voice and said, "But, Jesus Christ, you can't ride the freights in winter."

"Well I am", I responded, "and I just thought I could bunk down in your room tonight, Karl. If that's Ok."

"Jesus Christ", his favourite expletive, "of course it's alright", said the boss, recovering his authority.

And then the incredible repetition, "I suppose you're hungry".

"Of course", I said.

"Then Ok! Get in the car and let's go and meet the folks."

His wife gave me a warm welcome in her own quiet way. His two daughters, considerably changed, both now secretaries in Government offices, sure of themselves, but along with Peter, fascinated by the stories of my travels and forthcoming journey home. I glowed in their warmth, and refused to think of tomorrow and the real cold. It did leave me a little concerned. The boss had kept niggling away during the evening; he kept repeating, "Nobody rides the freights in the winter, it's too dangerous." After a very convivial and nostalgic evening, I said my goodbyes and caught a streetcar back to the workshop.

Karl was a talker; his English might be hard to follow, but it never stopped him arguing or making a point. He was a patriot and proud of it. If anyone suggested that Germans and Austrians were the same, he became agitated and heated and resisted such opinions vehemently. Whereas George, the upholsterer, was German, antagonistically German. He belonged to the local Nazi party that operated within the large German colony in Regina. He had been questioned many times by the Mounties for distributing inflammatory literature, but he remained indifferent. Many a heated political discussion took place in the workshop between them.

But now Karl had some beer, and we reminisced into the early hours.

A few hours' sleep. I was up early, and by daybreak had wandered down to the railroad. It was very cold, grey skies, with a covering of packed snow on the ground. I was stomping up and down to keep warm beside some stationary flat cars and cattle trucks. I should have known better than to be within sight of the station.

A locomotive was shunting cars back and forth, and when the train was assembled I knew it would be heading east. Except for this train crew there wasn't a soul to be seen. But I had become careless, and of course I would have been conspicuous from the apparently deserted station.

Then unexpectedly, I saw a large figure emerge from the side of the building, and stride purposefully in my direction. A moment of irrational frustration, then panic. A railway cop, a big man - they always seemed big, maybe it was the long heavy coats. I strode quickly away, he started running, so did I… muttering to myself as I did so, "What an idiot! You should have known better, standing there in full view, you've had enough experience; serves you right for being so stupid." And running wasn't very easy, wearing so much clothing. Fortunately I was young and fit, the gap widened and he soon gave up. I was still talking to myself about paying the price of carelessness when I stopped running.

The cop had sorely damaged my confidence. I couldn't possibly go back, and by now I was too far away from town, though on the east of it, to catch a train, as by the time it reached me it would be travelling far too fast for one to jump. Anyhow my nerve was gone, luck had deserted me. I was at a low ebb.

I walked disconsolately along the rail tracks, then came to where the highway crossed the railroad. And abruptly thought, walking won't get me home, let's try hitch hiking.

This was No.1 Highway which ran right across the prairies, east and west, and from this point the next large town would be Brandon in Manitoba, about two hundred and fifty miles away, then another one hundred and fifty miles to Winnipeg.

Regina was already back in the distance as I stepped out onto the hard packed snow surface of the road, and left the rail tracks behind.

Few people hitch hiked in winter in Canada, and away from the towns traffic was sparse. But motorists invariably stopped and offered lifts, without the need for thumbing. Providing there were cars on the road. As I walked I could see miles in front and miles behind, empty, flat and grey. I kept looking back and would have seen a car from far away. It was quite pleasant walking, but in these vast spaces, ridiculously slow.

Then it happened! Way in the distance behind me was a black speck, disappearing, then reappearing with the undulations of the road. And for a long time, as I kept looking back, seeming to get no nearer. But now it is distinct, and the tempo of the engine has changed. It *is* slowing down. It draws alongside me, a voice calls out, "Want a lift, buddy? I'm going forty miles east on the highway." A middle aged man was leaning toward me.

"Thanks Guv!", I said. And within minutes my circumstances had changed.

I was now sitting beside the driver, going east at sixty miles an hour. Homeward once more.

The Canadian farmer, like most farmers everywhere was uncommunicative; a few questions, "Where are you going, son?", he asked. I rambled on quite willingly. But somehow his lack of real interest dried me up, a few more desultory words about the weather, then silence.

However I was warm and comfortable, and my confidence was returning as we approached the small town of Fort Quappelle. "I'm turning off here", said my taciturn driver, and awoke me from my dreaming. Fort Quappelle was reminding me of my first job after I had arrived in Canada.

I had been sent to a farmer not many miles from here. When he met me at the station he said, "I'm Mr. Turner, but call me Joe." This business of calling people by their christian names was alien to me, (adults were Mr. at home) and took a long time to adapt to.

On arrival at his farm, he informed me that he had hired me to go with him about a hundred and fifty miles south, near the American border, where he had purchased a half section of land, virgin prairie, some fifteen miles from the small town of Trossachs.

He intended to "break", i.e. plough, as much as possible during the following month, and that I would be picking stones ahead of his plough. In the following two days I was taught how to harness, to hitch, and to drive a team - two - of heavy horses. They would be my responsibility for the month we would be away. Joe's wife and an older hired hand would run the farm in the meantime.

We left early one morning. Joe, driving a tractor with a raised plough behind, and I, with my team of horses, hitched to a wagon loaded with all the things we would need for a month.

For three days, stopping with friendly farmers overnight, we plodded through this flat, quiet, and empty land, living largely on bread, beans and salt pork. We eventually arrived at a farmhouse owned by a Swedish farmer and family, beside whose land Joe had purchased his half square mile.

One could hardly imagine a more exposed site. A wooden Dutch style farmhouse, and a similar barn, set in the emptiest landscape possible. Flat, semi arid, treeless and bushless. Hot, with the sun glaring down from an immense sky, and add to that the *SILENCE*. To a lad, fresh out from the "Smoke", I think it was the palpable feel of the silence that weighed more heavily on me. A dog barked, a cow mooed, *that* was a noise, that was apparent. Then… *SILENCE*.

Joe had arranged with the Swede for us to live temporarily in a small wooden shed, and our team of horses to use his corral. Joe would drive the tractor all day. I would use the team and wagon, plus crowbar and chains, and clear the land of rocks. Covering a swathe of land ahead of the ploughing.

At midday I was to return to the hut, feed and water the horses, prepare myself some food, then take food and coffee out to Joe. Then continue working until evening. Again, after tending the horses, prepare food for a late supper.

The farmer - call me Olaf - had a few cows and hens, so the basic foods were supplied by him, including bread and potatoes; this, added to the tinned food we had brought with us became our regular diet.

The work was very hard. I had a ravenous appetite and could, and did, eat everything and anything. Tomatoes, which I had never been able to stomach, out of tins, became delicious. On the first day Joe had said, "When it's about noon, walk over to the fence wire. When the shadow of the posts run into each other that's noon". Neither of us had watches, and that was my first understanding of every direction being taken from a geographical point of view. Back home, we had gone to left or right, twisting about endlessly, seldom with any sense of latitude or longitude. But here all roads ran east and west, north and south. An obstacle had indeed to be big to alter that. All farms were laid out in square grids, so obviously all directions, when asked, were referred to by the points of the compass. Hence the use of fence posts at midday. A rudimentary sundial.

Also, to add some sense of time: fifteen miles away ran the railroad, a branch line that appeared to be used only twice a day. Once in the morning and again later in the afternoon. Then that melancholy wail, that double "Ooee - Ooee", of the train's hooter wafting faintly across the distance, adding to the sense of wilderness and vastness. But, at least informing one that time still mattered.

All day long I picked stones from the surface, I dug up rocks, and when they were too big, levered them up with a crowbar, worked chains around them, hitched the team of horses to the chains and towed them to

15

the boundary. All the smaller ones were loaded in the wagon, and again when full, taken to the boundary wire; where within a few days I was steadily building a rock wall.

Joe's problem was the unseen one. Those stones that lay just below the surface. All day he sat on his tractor, driving, his eyes fixed on the land just ahead of him. Any suspicion of underground stone, generally by noticing the grass thinning, he would raise his plough shares and skim the surface. But he missed a number of times: a sudden bang and clatter behind him, and a plough share had hit rock and fractured. Then there was the time consuming job of removing that particular share and replacing it with a new one.

At the end of our first week, Joe borrowed Olaf's truck, and drove the fifteen miles to the nearest town. All these small settlements were called towns, though all they consisted of generally, was a railway station, one or two grain elevators, a few houses and maybe a general store. This one, Trossachs, did have a blacksmith to whom Joe took his damaged shares, and spent most of the day kicking his heels in sheer frustration at so much wasted time.

Joe was not a talker. A word here and there about work, the horses, the food, invariably chewing a stem of grass. But after two weeks, more comments about the weather, worrying comments, "About time it rained", he would say, or "'Bout time that Chinook brought rain." The Chinook, a warm south westerly wind, had been blowing for days, not fierce, a steady breeze, like a draught from out of a hot oven. Not warm, hot!, sending the temperature throughout the day above a hundred degrees Fahrenheit.

Normally rain would come from that direction, but not this time.

Joe had been foreseeing in one important respect. On our first day he had produced two straw sombreros, saying, "You'll need one of these, can't be bareheaded out in the field, you'll get sunstroke."

I had never worn anything on my head before, but I was adapting fast to many things, and I soon grew to like my big hat.

Olaf had a wife and two young children, but they were only seen at a distance, shyly. Olaf would come over with a pitcher of buttermilk and ask me many questions about the "Old Country". I don't think he was really interested in the answers, it was my cockney accent that intrigued him, "Never heard anyone talk like you, they all talk like that in England?"

But as we entered our third week, Olaf, like Joe, was becoming increasingly worried. This was late June, and his acres of wheat and barley were wilting. Now he would only talk or think of rain, or the lack of it. The spectre of a real drought was frightening.

There was a dull, voiceless anxiety expressed in his face as he watched his crop begin to burn and wither.

The end of three weeks.

Joe just sat one evening, gazing vacantly across the prairie. Lately the plough had not been working right. When he had first started ploughing, it was dreamlike to watch the five ploughshares turn the virgin sod, smoothly, silkily, deeply. But now, when even the tough prairie grass was turning brown the ground had become dry and hard, he could no longer plough deep. The tractor was fighting the good earth but no longer subduing it.

The sun would not be denied. The Chinook had died, but no rain came. A hot stillness prevailed, and Joe was seeing his plans, his dreams, fading inexorably away.

He looked at me suddenly. "We will pack up and go back home tomorrow. Heck! You can't fight that blasted dry sod." The longest sentence I had ever heard from him.

He had assumed that if one worked hard, all the hours that God sent, one must succeed. But the sun had laughed derisively down on him and now he faced failure.

I just said, "Ok Guv!". I had no way of expressing regret or understanding and, in a sense, had become like him. Talking little, but enjoying the hard manual labour. I had acquired a tan like an Indian. My hands were calloused, and I was strong with solid muscles and proud of my physical ability.

However we were going back…

Early the following morning Olaf came over to see us off. He had that far away look that comes into the eyes of a person who faces defeat. His crops shrivelling in front of him, and nothing on earth could he do about it. He was beyond words, he managed, "Have a good ride", turned and left us.

A steady plod for the next three days, through the hot dry landscape, a dawning realisation that I hadn't seen rain for weeks, and an awareness of what a good old English rainy day was worth, or would be if it could be transported here.

Joe had a regular "hired man", so I was hardly surprised when a few days later he said, "Sorry, son, but I can't keep you on."

So, with twelve dollars, one month's wages in my pocket, I was "on the road". My first experience of farming and I was still not seventeen. This month's introduction to farming was not auspicious…

***

In Fort Quappelle I once again bought a loaf of bread, ate some, disposing of the rest in my pockets as I headed back to the highway. Once again walking east. The sun was shining now, the snow crisp, and somehow I was happier. Though I had to admit the pace was ridiculous. But something would turn up. I had lost my earlier depression now that I was fifty miles beyond Regina.

Sure enough, very soon there was a steady *clip clop* coming up behind me. A farmer, muffled in his sheepskin coat, driving a team of horses with a wagon on sleighs.

"Jump up, Bud", he said, as they drew level, taking it for granted that anybody walking required a lift.

I did so, but with considerable doubts in my mind; it was late morning now, and the chances of getting a lift in a car were good. Whereas I was travelling now at about ten miles an hour, and I wondered how long for. My mind was soon put to rest, for this farmer was very different from the average. Talkative, questioning. Where was I going? How? Where had I worked, and so on.

He had a farm ten miles further on, and his pride shone through as he eulogised about his brick farmhouse, his brick barn, and all the modern innovations he had, that were so rare on the prairie. Even tap water and a flush toilet. He waxed eloquent, but so involved me in his conversation that it made me immediately at home with him.

Probably an hour flew by, when he said, "There it is", and his pride was justified. By the north side of the highway, set back a hundred yards from the road, with a windbreak belt of conifer trees encircling it on three sides, a large white gate facing us on the south side, was his elegant red brick house, a prairie home with a difference. Civilisation set in a snowy waste.

He halted his horses, and was silent for a moment. Then gave me a quizzical look, and unexpectedly said, "Say, son, why not stop right here, work for me, you don't need to go back to old England. We would get on well, how about it?"

I was taken by surprise, the first time in five years I had actually been offered a job and home without having to chase it. And feeling so akin to the man. The look on his face, he could have been my Dad. But I was travelling east. No longer did the pundits cry "Go west, young man, go west." The west now, was depressed and uninviting, and anyhow - I was going home.

"Sorry, Bud", I said to the farmer, "Thanks for the offer and the ride, but I'm going home."

"Ok, son. Good luck", he replied as I jumped down from the wagon and started walking.

I was elated, I had a spring in my step, somebody had softened, not everybody was tough and hard. A man had offered me a job and home. I kept repeating it as I walked on. It was not believable, of course, with a shrug it was in the abstract. But that glow persisted.

Few cars had passed whilst I was with the farmer. And now, once again the road in front or behind disappeared to a point of nothingness…

A straight empty ribbon as far as the eye could see, and as I walked, I kept looking back…

After a while there was a black speck behind me, on the horizon. Most likely a car, still miles away, but coming in the right direction. Before long the speck became a large black car appearing to be travelling at speed. I kept glancing back, no doubt now, I could hear its powerful engine.

I knew how conspicuous I must be, alone, on a deserted highway miles from anywhere. And now I was subconsciously listening for the motor to change its tone, indicating it was slowing down. A sigh of relief… opportunity knocks, as I heard the change of tempo, and a car braking beside me.

A terse, "Wanna lift?", from the driver, an equally short, "Thanks pal!", from me. And I was inside.

"I'm going to Brandon", he said.

"Fine by me", I replied as I settled into the comfort of upholstered leather seats, and the warm atmosphere of a heated interior. This I could learn to enjoy.

A few words from me regarding the weather, an indifferent response, and as he leaned forward over the wheel the car quickly regained its speed. Whether he liked driving fast, or was in a hurry, I never knew, but common sense told me there would be no conversation as I glanced at the speedometer which was now steady at ninety miles an hour, and if maintained would bring us to Brandon within about two hours.

The road, although No.1 Highway, had only a gravel surface, and graders were a common sight, thus keeping the corrugations that would normally form, levelled out.

For a slow car it was a bumpy ride. Once the vehicle passed a certain speed the ride became smooth and now the feeling of gliding was quickly relaxing and I recalled a very different ride I had taken a year previously.

It was late fall, I had no work and no money. I was in Calgary and decided to catch a "freight" to Edmonton. I had never been to Edmonton, which was two hundred miles away, north, and a bit off the beaten track, but felt like the majority of transients who were eternally boasting of where they had been. So maybe a new name was at the end of the rainbow. At least somewhere different to visit.

Some hobos had travelled the railroads, over the whole of North America. It had become a way of life. Work was very scarce, but contradictorily people were very generous, and providing one was willing to ask, there was no need for anyone to go hungry.

Throughout the summer months, the waste land around the railroad freight yards was often a temporary headquarters for the hobos, among whose fraternity they were known as "The Jungles". This is where they gathered before boarding trains in their continuous search for a greener land, or some vague, wistful El Dorado, that only existed in their minds. But they were tough, of necessity, and train crews preferred not to see them, though the half million men wandering across Canada right through the thirties could not be missed, as they sat on top of box cars, or filled the doorways of empty ones. Ever on the move, with thousands of miles of sparsely populated space to travel in. Only in the large towns or cities did they need to worry about the police. Obviously for the great majority there was little option, though in a peculiar way maybe it was an extension of the pioneer spirit of their forefathers, who were now willing to "move on", to seek something better. Completely selfish in their individual searching for they didn't know what.

They were quite willing to "bum", they never thought of it as begging. "Can you spare a dime, Bud? Can you spare a cigarette, pal?". Common enough demands around the poorer parts of towns. And people did give. There was a philosophical attitude at the time. "But for the grace of God."

There was a dull, inarticulate understanding that somewhere, something was radically wrong, and that anybody could be dragged down by this inexplicable depression which appeared to have no end.

All these hobos were going somewhere, if one asked. "Sure, I'm heading for Vancouver, heard there was work there." "Yes, Sir, I'm going to Toronto." "Say, Buddy! I'm off north to Edmonton, do a bit of lumbering", and so on. They all thought their journeying was leading to somewhere, there must be something at the end of the line. Life must have a purpose!

Though as a long freight pulled slowly through some small prairie town, with maybe a score or so hobos sitting idly on top, the local cop would often be seen walking beside the train, constantly repeating, "There's nothing here, keep moving". The hobos would seldom respond, they had heard it too often, they remained impassively seated, watching the cop enigmatically as the train crawled slowly towards the next town. And who knows, work! Opportunity! Life!

At the bigger, well known "jungles", a fire would be kept burning. Coffee would be simmering blackly in a large soot-encrusted can. The hobos said, "When a horseshoe could stand up in it, it was strong enough". And somebody would be pushing potatoes among the ashes.

But far more important, there was always somebody who knew when a train would be pulling out, and its destination. And equally important, which town had the worst railway cops.

I wandered down to the "jungle" and joined a group of men idling their time away, doing nothing in particular, talking, smoking, and passing the inevitable can of coffee around. I never did acquire a taste for that thick black liquid they called coffee. But nevertheless, I drank, and passed tobacco around, entering into the aimless conversation.

Soon discovering that a freight left for the north later in the day.

A few hours later, a group of us decided to catch it, after a while drifting over the lines towards where a big black locomotive was shunting all kinds of rail wagons back and forth, building itself gradually to a great length.

We were standing, semi hidden amongst a variety of stationary box cars and wagons, just watching the process of a massive freight train being created, and also keeping a wary eye open over the area in general, as railway cops had an unpleasant habit of appearing from nowhere, particularly when a freight was due to leave.

But not this time. The train was now complete, with only a gentle hissing of steam from the engine, as the rail men took their allotted places. The pause was like the moment before a team of horses are set to take the strain of a heavy load.

Suddenly, once again that Banshee wail, as the hooter gave out that forlorn, long sound that signalled it was off, and as it took the strain, the couplings clanking and juddering, the wheels slipping, as the whole monstrous length of the train stuttered into motion. But within a few minutes a slow steady pull as hundreds of wagons rolled smoothly on their way.

This was the moment when we all left our hiding places, ran across the rails, and started running alongside the train, seeking empty unlocked box cars. The speed as yet, was comfortable, and as they passed one could note whether the cars were locked or empty. But the end of the train was approaching, and realising there were no empties, one by one we grabbed the iron stanchion, swung ourselves up onto the plate above the couplings, then up the metal rungs and onto the roofs of the box cars.

One could ride on top, but when the train gathered speed it would be cold and uncomfortable, and anyhow, surely there's an "empty" somewhere along its length.

We walked along the top, on the foot wide boardwalk that extended from end to end of each car. By the time we drew near the locomotive we were no longer walking, but crawling on hands and knees, as by now the train's speed was such that the cars swayed slightly from side to side, and walking had therefore become very risky.

Of course there were always those carefree wanderers who trotted along, jumping from car to car, indifferent to danger, and generally grinning exultantly as they did so. They were the hardened transients whose whole way of life had become geared to "just moving on".

Just before we reached the engine, only two box cars back from the tender, we could see an empty slatted cattle truck. We could also see that it was unlocked. I brought up the rear, following the others as they slowly climbed down between the wagons, and then crawled or edged sideways along the slats. The first one to reach the door jiggled it open, allowing the door to swing on its hinges. Then one after another we were inside. I being the last, pulled the door closed behind me.

It was an improvement from being outside, a sound floor and roof, but the sides very much open to the elements. Under such circumstances we did the only thing possible, sat down with our backs to the engine, and slipped into a trance-like condition, relaxed because no one had control of events. "So what, Buddy, take it easy, life goes on." The very motion of the train itself was hypnotic and soothing, as the miles slipped away behind us.

A few hours passed, then we began clattering over points as we entered the environs of Edmonton. The speed lessened.

It was late evening now, and the lights of the city were spreading ahead as we jogged about to chase the chill from our bones, and to prepare for the jump and roll, before getting too near the outskirts of the city and the danger of "cops".

The rails began to multiply as we went past many sidings. Then as we came to a suitable embankment one after the other we jumped and rolled expertly, and with much experience down the bank, without harm and now wide awake. No cops about, no danger, as we brushed ourselves down. A few words as we went our separate ways towards the lights.

A sudden realisation of how hungry I was, and what to do about it? Too late for the Salvation Army, too late for bumming, and it would be unwise to knock on doors this late. No sign of a "jungle" here - getting too late in the year!

Only one other alternative, the Police station…

The cops were a pain in the neck when chasing or accosting one. But the stations were modern and warm, and some of the travellers had had a lucky experience with sympathetic officers. I had certainly never been in a station before, but the alternatives seemed non existent.

So, I walked briskly towards the city centre, but when I saw the blue light, and the conspicuous sign above the door of a large imposing brick building I wanted to hesitate, but knew I dared not, otherwise my nerve would go.

Putting, as I hoped, an expressionless look on my face, I walked boldly in.

A quiet empty foyer. Just one officer sitting at a desk, casually glancing through a magazine, who glanced up and gave me a long blank look as I walked towards him, quaking inwardly but trying hard not to show it.

"Yes", he said. I didn't really know what to say. Some of my companions of the road had acquired a technique, a phrase or two to explain themselves when faced with a similar awkward situation. I had no pet phrase or any sophistication. All I could respond with, as unemotionally as I thought, as circumstances would allow was, "I haven't had anything to eat today, I've no money, and nowhere to sleep".

A grunt, a long silence as he continued to flick the pages of his magazine, then, "Where did you come from today?" I explained. "You English?", again I agreed. A few more questions about my background, then, "Wait here." And he disappeared through a door into a back room. I could hear faint voices.

He quickly returned and said, "Well, it's a quiet night tonight, no drunks; like a warm cell for the night?" With a sigh of relief I replied, "Yes, thanks", as he said, "Come this way", and led me downstairs and unlocked the door of a heated cell, complete with bunk and mattress, and washbasin. Luxury to me, at least I was out of the cold for one night.

"I'll be back shortly", he said. And sure enough, ten minutes later he returned with a large mug of tea in one hand, and an enormous plate stacked with bread and butter, plus a blob of jam on the side, brusquely saying, "Ok, son, see you in the morning." And the door was slammed. A lucky break! But if I had hesitated at the entrance, fortune would not have favoured me. When times are hard even luck has to be fought for.

I slept like a log, solid!

The key in the lock in the morning awakened me. The same officer, with a repeat offering of mug of tea, a mountain of bread and butter, and a query, "Sleep well?". "Like a log", I replied, eyeing the food. My morale taking another leap upwards. "Right, get through that, I'll be back in half an hour."

When he returned he said, "Ok, bud, let's go", as he walked me upstairs to the foyer and entrance. "Look, son, don't let's see you again, have to run you in as a vagrant." But a gentle punch on the arm as he said it, and he was gone.

I had no intention of getting out of town just yet. I've come to Edmonton, let's see something of it. I was born in Edmonton, London, England. And it appeared strange, that apparently in the early part of the nineteenth century this city was named after my birthplace, simply because a clerk, working in the original trading post decided to call it that, since he also was born in my birthplace.

It is situated near one of the old Hudson's Bay fur trading posts, on the North Saskatchewan river, and so has a little longer history than most prairie cities.

It was a fine day as I wandered around, eventually arriving at the tabernacle.

The Salvation Army was well established in all major towns and cities, and the "Sally Ally", as it was affectionately called, had a very good reputation for its care of wanderers and down-and-outs. A hall or reception area had facilities for minor indoor amusements, with tables and chairs catering for those who just wanted somewhere to pass an hour away, and meet and chat with those of a similar disposition.

At the enquiry cubbyhole I was informed that as I was an unknown stranger I could have a bunk free, for one night. But if I stayed around it would cost ten cents a night thereafter, and then only for a maximum of three nights, as they were not a hotel as such, but merely trying to help those who were ever on the move. Soup, bread and tea was served twice a day to anybody who needed it, without question.

So now, I could relax, play some table tennis, and have a few games of chequers with "Old George".

"Old George" had apparently sat in his corner for ever. At least he looked like a permanent fixture, with a chequer board set up on a table in front of him.

He took on all comers, and had a reputation of being a very good player; no one could beat "Old George", was the consensus of opinion. He was a grey haired man, probably in his fifties, and to most of us "old". Granddad, most of them called him.

I said, "I'll give you a game, George." "Ok, sit down", he replied. He was quiet and unobtrusive, and with methodical deliberation he wiped the board with me. I had prided myself I could play "Draughts", as I knew it. But after three ignominious defeats I retired, and left "Old George" awaiting another opponent, puffing away at an old pipe in his own snug corner.

Later in the day, two newcomers breezed in. One, a big aggressive type, called out as he entered, "Hi, you guys, I'm Brian." A few muttered "Hi", but mostly they were silent. There was an immediate tenseness, a guarded atmosphere, an instinctive dislike.

He talked briefly, and loudly to a number of men. Then noticing George comfortably puffing away, walked over to him saying, "Nice little corner you've got here, granddad. Want a game of chequers?" "Suits me, sit down", George responded. "Haven't got time", said the newcomer, as he just stood, looking down patronisingly on George, with his little games table. "You move first", he said. The board was always set up and ready, and everybody thought, "Old George will bring him down one". But to everybody's dismay, after a series of "Take this, go on, take that", George was hopelessly beaten.

Brian went to walk away, but George said, "Give me a chance to get my own back."

"Up to you, Granddad, set them up. You're a glutton for punishment."

By now, everyone had gathered around, willing George to win. But all the moral support in the world made no difference. George's defeat was complete and humiliating, and we all avoided meeting his eye for a long time after.

However, a little later Brian said to his friend, "Let's go". He had ridden roughshod over "poor old George". We hated him. And yet, heck! He knew his game, he sure did! It made one almost jealous of such superiority.

I soon became friendly with a French Canadian of about my own age, Maurice. He had been on the road a very long time, and had no wish to do anything else. The second day he said, "Let's get some money".

We went to an ordinary residential district, knocked on the door and asked for food. When we knocked on a door with this simple request we were seldom refused. Most times the lady - nine times out of ten it was a woman who answered - would say, "Wait." And a little later would come back with food of some kind, and not an unnecessary word would have been spoken. Just occasionally they would be curious about our circumstances and ask questions, and so, get into conversation. And also, although there was generally no refusal, there was often one sensed, an unease. We brought the depression home to them, while we were around it could not be ignored. Quite unintentionally we made them "think", and somehow they could no longer feel so secure themselves.

When we did come across someone who was interested and the conversation became easy, it was a simple matter to introduce the fact that we had nowhere to sleep that night. Invariably that heralded another "Wait a minute", and the lady returning with a dollar bill saying, "A bed for the night."

In some of the small seedy hotels a room for the night was only fifty cents, or a bed in a shared room for less than twenty-five cents. So, one dollar in this time of short money, was wealth.

Food was no problem, we often had too much!

After the first day we devised a system whereby, when Maurice had worked one side of a block and I the other, we would meet and memorise those houses we had obtained money from. And the next day he would call only on those I had got money from, and I his.

During the rest of the day we would spend time in the cinema, or a beer parlour. Or wandering around this attractive northern city, in the warm late Indian summer weather. A pleasant, casual but insecure existence, that quickly became boring.

And winter was just around the corner…

I was not surprised, when after a few days Maurice said, "I'm off west to Vancouver for the winter. Coming?"

I was becoming disillusioned with our way of life; going back to Calgary, then on to Vancouver did not really appeal, but what else? So unenthusiastically I agreed, and the following day found us back at the sidings.

No problems, we caught a freight, and after an uneventful ride we arrived back in Calgary.

The "jungle" was crowded with men of a like mind. It was well into October, there had been some severe frosts, and now the wide open prairie had lost its appeal. All the talk now was of the west coast.

Vancouver, and the west coast generally, had a wet but mild climate. Whereas the temperature on the plains would soon plummet, the prairie freeze-up would settle in, snow would fall, which would be added to constantly and remain until the spring.

Even casual work would cease; the few hired men the farmers employed during the growing season would now be adding to the mass of unemployed.

It was the system at the time with prairie farmers to take on hired help for the season, April to October. After harvest they would be paid off, with a "maybe see you next year". That was when there was a general exodus to the bright lights and the west coast. Some farmers offered their hired help board and roof for the winter, in return for such chores as chopping wood.

But when the harvest had been good or reasonable, most men with a season's pay in their pocket headed, along with the hobos east or west, to some city that appealed to them, and somehow survived the winter.

The general knowledge, drifting around the "jungle", was that in two hours - dusk by then - a freight would be pulling out for the west. Six hundred miles through the Rockies to the Pacific coast. A hazardous route with many tunnels, as the railroad twisted and turned on itself to gain height through the mountains.

Most of the men intending to go west, had ambled in, in ones and twos, towards the western end of the yards, taking advantage of idle railway vehicles to avoid being seen. We had seen no sign of cops, but the magnetic pull of Vancouver was so great at this time of year that the authorities concentrated on preventing, or trying to prevent this mass exodus.

Maurice and I were mingling with this scattered crowd, our nerves on edge.

There were the usual rows of stationary box cars, flat cars, carriages and dead engines, spread over a huge acreage of rails. It was odd, how everybody edged along the sides of these immobile vehicles, listening for the train that must soon depart. Ready to run and jump.

They all had done it many times before. That tense moment when that forlorn sound, the train hooter gave its warning of departure.

The engine crew were all aboard, the linesmen and general track workers all gone. The mournful double hoot came. The train commenced its journey, cars juddering, until in a few minutes it became a slow steady pull, and then we, with all the other hidden men, were running towards it.

But this time it was different. From the head of the train, seemingly from nowhere, there were figures running, half a dozen baton-swinging cops. Like the turning of the tide, the men, who a few minutes before were running towards the train, spun around and were immediately running in every other direction.

Every man for himself…

Each of us knew that to be caught or cornered by these vicious railway police, meant a beating at least. The consequences of which at times, reputably had been fatal, or one could be injured and just left lying.

I had never seen so many officers at one time. Out of the corner of my eye I saw Maurice, sprinting off to the left, being chased by a big heavy man, but Maurice was slight and very agile. I had seen him run along the top of moving box cars. No, he wasn't going to be caught.

I never did see him again.

In fact, I was sprinting the race of my life, fear adding wings to my feet. Without looking back I knew I was being chased, a sudden silent personal contest, my heart pounding. It seemed ages, but after a few minutes I sensed a widening of the gap between us. My panic began to subside, although I kept steadily running for a long time, across rails and waste ground; putting as much distance as possible between myself and those ominous batons.

The night had settled down, when at last I stopped and tried to recapture my reason. Stranded, in the middle of nowhere, cold, alone and demoralised. I had one dollar in my pocket, so I decided to wend my way back into town, find a bed, and call it a day.

***

The prospect ahead was daunting. I had a good map with me, so I knew there was nothing between me and the next small town, some thirty miles away. "So! Just keep moving, buddy", I said to myself; the times I had heard that! And now, that's all there is to do. *Walk, walk, walk.*

I settled down to a lively pace, and became engrossed with my thoughts, soon accepting that a long trudge was inevitable. Just forget about it, and remember that Regina, where I left that morning, is already over two hundred miles behind me.

I am in Manitoba and somewhere during the day I have left the Mountain Time Zone well behind me. Central Time Zone now, so I have actually gained an hour; though having no watch it makes little difference, but I will feel I have done well.

When I get to Winnipeg, *not if*, but when, I will have to readjust my means of travelling yet again.

31

About a hundred miles east of that city commences the great mass of the Canadian Shield. A thousand miles of rock and forest, extending to the tree line the barren lands, in the northern, relatively untouched wilderness. There are no roads east through this virtually uninhabited area. Only two railway lines, the Canadian Pacific and the Canadian National, cut right through into Ontario, skirting the Great Lakes, and connecting Eastern and Western Canada.

The trans Canada highway, still a dream in the planners' eyes.

So, beyond Manitoba's capital, I *had* to ride the freights once again. And always, nagging away at the back of my mind was the knowledge that the St Lawrence freezes up in winter. The last Atlantic liners leave Montreal somewhere around mid December, and I was banking on being there before that happened. After that, until the spring, the big ships only came to Halifax, Nova Scotia. I had steadfastly refused to face up to that possibility. Montreal itself was still incredibly far away, and Halifax! Probably nine hundred miles beyond that.

No… Fate couldn't be that unkind.

I said a little prayer as I plodded steadily on, then glanced up at that myriad of stars, and instantly, there was a wave of light across the sky. A curtain of green and white, unfolding to the horizon. Slowly at first, as the Northern Lights - the famous Aurora Borealis - gave their ballet show. This spectacle I had often seen before in the past four years. Sometimes merely a few flashing lights. But this time, like a concert in the night sky. A shimmering, silent, rolling motion; beginning in the north, and extending fast, then slow, across the whole expanse of sky. A cascade, then retreating to a small pink glow in the north, then just as suddenly repeating itself, like something alive, but eerily silent.

This continued for maybe an hour. The only sound being the scrunch of my boots on the hard packed snow, as I doggedly devoured the miles through the still unchanging scenery.

No cars had passed for a long time now; I had given up expecting any, let alone the hope of getting a lift. I had no watch, so time, under the circumstances was a matter of guesswork.

There were two small hamlets between Brandon and Corberry, the next small town. So when I passed a little cluster of houses with an odd light showing here and there, but lifeless, I could estimate how far I had walked. I had studied my map carefully, and knew that beyond the last hamlet I had about ten miles to go to Corberry, the small town I was relying on.

After passing the second group of houses I guessed it was between nine and ten o'clock. Striding the empty road and still occasionally breaking and eating a piece of bread I felt as if I could walk for ever. At times I was humming parts of my favourite hillbilly song.

The wheels hummed a song as the train rolled along,
And the black smoke came pouring from its stack.

How many times had we sung that around the old piano in the Barton house, I mused, as I slowly covered the miles. And tomorrow I must be back on the freights again.

It must be about midnight. I think I can see the shadowy forms of buildings silhouetted against the sky ahead. The grain elevators, even at night stood out in the distance. Two or three of these huge buildings, a hundred feet high and painted a universal brick red, were the trademark of all prairie towns. Cathedrals of the plains, someone called them, and they dominated the few small houses clustered about, and were the very essence of life for the grain growing farmers.

Every town from Eastern Manitoba to Western Alberta, the whole vast expanse of the Canadian prairies relied on them for their very existence. Plus the network of railways that connected them to the outside world.

I am flagging as I enter the small town of Corberry, abruptly aware of how many miles I have walked.

It is absolutely quiet, not a light to be seen. But within a few minutes a man is advancing toward me, and I instinctively know this must be the local policeman.

Many small towns have one resident "cop", and this town would appear to qualify. In the silence the crunch of my boots on the hard packed snow would have been heard a long way off.

"Hi, Bud, where have you come form?", he greeted me.

"Brandon", I replied.

"Brandon? That's thirty miles away", he queried.

"I know that *too*, I've just walked it, and I'm looking for a small hotel where I can get a bed for the night", I responded hopefully. "I didn't get a lift", I added resentfully.

"Of course you wouldn't get a lift coming out of Brandon. You passed the Provincial mental hospital, nobody gives a lift in that area! Anyhow, we have a small hotel, I'll show you". And fell in step beside me.

Not many people walked into his town in the middle of the night, and certainly never in mid December!

He questioned me as to where I was going, about how, and why and when. I was an unusual type of traveller, and he was most certainly intrigued. Of course I explained my fare money awaited me in Montreal and that I only had a few dollars on my person to get me there.

After a couple of hundred yards we arrived - it always seemed incredible that these small prairie towns, with only two or three hundred population, generally had a small hotel. I was relieved to see the little reception area was lit, and the receptionist-cum-owner was lounging, smoking, in a comfortable armchair.

The cop, a really friendly guy, could not resist saying immediately, "Say, Frank, what do you know. This young Englishman has just walked in from Brandon, and I mean *walked*. And he reckons to go to London, and I mean London, England. Struth! I guess you've got a spare bed."

Frank, the proprietor, an ordinary looking, quiet, middle-aged man said, "Sure, son, come this way".

The sudden, unexpected warmth of the central heating made me quite languorous as I followed him upstairs. He unlocked a door, said, "Have a good sleep", and was gone.

Ten minutes later, after a quick wash, I was asleep, or was I? No doubt, being overtired but unaware of it. I seemed to be involved in running. There was this big ship slowly pulling away from the dock; I had to catch it, but couldn't close the gap between us. I was puffing, puffing, running, then gradually there was a space appearing between ship and harbour. My feet were no longer on the ground. I was flying. I must reach it.

I shuddered and woke up sweating…

I hadn't consciously been worrying about arriving in Montreal before the big freeze up, but I lay there, awake for a while knowing that the possibilities were very real.

I spent a very restless night and was up at seven; it was still dark outside as I splashed cold water over myself to liven me up.

I dressed for the outside, then went downstairs to the reception area.

Frank was sitting in his armchair smoking and reading a paper. The policeman was at the far side of the room, in a small dining annexe, drinking coffee with another man.

"Good morning, Guv", I said to Frank. "How much do I owe you for the room?", sweating that it wouldn't be too much.

"Have some breakfast", he replied.

"No, thanks, must get on the road."

Then the cop called out, "Come over here and get some coffee."

I was ravenous; yesterday's loaf of bread was a long time ago, so, as if hypnotised, I took a seat beside him whilst he poured a cup of coffee, and again I responded to the incessant questions he fired at me. Particularly about how I was continuing beyond Winnipeg.

After a few minutes chattering, a door at the back opened, and a middle-aged, grey haired woman appeared, smiling; she placed a full breakfast in front of me, saying, "Enjoy that." Eggs, bacon, sausages, toast.

"Heck!", I was thinking as I devoured the lot in double quick time. "In for a penny, in for a pound."

Whilst I had been eating, my friendly officer had never stopped talking. But as I finished and rose to go he said, "Just one piece of advice, son, watch out for the railway police in Winnipeg, they're not nice."

"Now, how much do I owe you, Guv?", I asked, as I walked toward Frank, still with a terrible doubt. It might even be five dollars from my meagre few. On the other hand, my stomach was very content, and would not be reminding me of "its" needs for many more hours.

"That's Ok, son, on your way; good luck, hope you get to England for Christmas."

Strange, how a single generous gesture can throw one. My air of casual bravado was punctured abruptly. I was left speechless.

"Thanks. Thanks very much", I managed to say, as I walked out into the sunny but bitterly cold weather. Still feeling emotional and very vulnerable as I tried to adjust and calm myself, as once again I stepped out to the east.

My mood changed violently as within ten minutes, a large truck eased up beside me and a friendly voice called out, "Want a lift, Bud?" Speedily and happily I jumped up.

"Where you heading?", he asked, "Winnipeg", I replied.

"You're in luck, pal, that's where this old truck's going." It was early morning, about a hundred and fifty miles to the big city, so even this old boneshaker of a truck should get us there by midday.

Winnipeg is the largest and oldest of the prairie cities. It appears to stretch over a vast area, very straggly on the outskirts. Its age, like everything else in the west, is relevant only to the west. Fort Garry, a Hudson's Bay trading post on the Red River on which Winnipeg is founded, was only built in the 1820s.

But its favourable position on the eastern edge of the great plains meant it developed quickly, as settlers poured through to the west and spread steadily across the prairie provinces. It was the gateway to the west,

36

and earlier the "west" was synonymous with enterprise and opportunity, hence the oft repeated, "Go west, young man, go west!" But The Great Depression of the early thirties had altered all that.

Few farmers were political, they were independent, worked all the hours possible, reaped their harvests, and life was good.

Markets did not really bother them - until the 1930s.

***

I remember Mr. Gustav Larsen, a Swede. A name I had never heard before, and one I would not forget. He was short, broad, and strong as an ox. Proud of the amount of work he could accomplish, and he expected everybody else to do likewise.

His wife, also a Swede, was named Venka. A name I could never use. For that matter I could never call Mr. Larsen "Gus", as he suggested when we first met. Mrs. Larsen was also big, buxom and strong, with two young children, the boy eleven, the girl twelve. They both had all the makings of their parents, and were fortified by the huge meals their mother provided.

I had a great appetite, but in no way could I compete with the enormous quantities of food they all devoured. I was of slight build, and they were always pressing me to eat more. "You need more flesh, eat more, it will make you strong", was a common admonition, especially from Mrs. Larsen.

Gustav had taken me on. "I'll hire you for a month or two", he had said, "See how we get on."

I had just had my seventeenth birthday, July, and I had been in Canada only a couple of months. My first experience of farming, "hiring out", had been unsuccessful to say the least. The fact that the drought in the southern plains was largely responsible, hardly helped.

Gustav's farm was a hundred miles north of Regina, in parkland type of country on the northern fringes of the prairies, undulating land with sloughs and many wooded areas, and this year, unaffected by lack of rain.

Life on the farm was ritualistic.

We rose each morning at five thirty, and went to bed at nine thirty, and most of the time between was working time. I was taught how to harness and assemble an outfit of five horses, to hitch them to harrows, then sit well behind them on a small metal seat, and to feel the strength of those five horses pulling in unison. However within a couple of weeks of starting work harvest commenced, Gustav with a binder and four horse outfit. This implement cut and bound the wheat into sheaves, which it then disgorged onto the ground as it went along. My job was to follow the binder, setting the sheaves together to form stooks. This was very hard work: he had a good crop, with heavy sheaves, and during the course of the day I slipped a long way behind.

As the sun was sliding into the west, Venka would come out and join me, and by the time it was dark we would complete the stooking, then go back to the house for supper. This went on for days and weeks. And once again I got used to hard work and little else.

At meal times, or late evenings, conversation revolved entirely around farm life. There was a weekly newspaper, *'The Prairie Farmer'*, which in turn addressed itself largely to farmers' interests and problems. I quickly acquired knowledge and an interest in domestic animals, crops, and particularly at that time, market prices. They had plummeted right through the summer as the depression had deepened.

Gustav produced a good crop that year, and I well remember early in September, he was off to town with his first wagonload of wheat from the recent harvest.

Wheat was the basic produce, it seemed all prices were governed by it. The previous year two dollars a bushel was the average price. The norm! But this was 1930, and everybody was struggling to come to terms with the collapse of the economy, something which was entirely out of everyone's experience and understanding.

Gustav, with his load of sixty bushels of grain, drove off early that momentous morning for the twenty mile trip to town. He was unsure and subdued. The tales of collapsing prices were frightening, even of grain being refused at the elevators because of the glut.

He returned late in the day. His face, his attitude, morose and unbelieving. He had received thirty-five cents a bushel for his sixty bushels of wheat, an eighty per cent drop from the previous year. And still he could not believe what was happening; this was an unimaginable catastrophe.

But Gustav, never very talkative, became very articulate that night. He knew who was responsible! The newspapers throughout the summer had been printing news of the Russians dumping cut-price grain on the European market, particularly Britain, so spoiling the market for American and Canadian cereal farmers.

I knew nothing at all about Russo-Swedish history, but that evening I had an unexpected and unforgettable lesson on Swedish history. Gustav had found his scapegoat, and the words sprang from the adrenalin produced by emotion. So an inarticulate man became amazingly lucid, maybe not reasonable, but certainly lucid.

As he spoke, all the hated past from the previous century to the present day, up surged. How the Russians had fought with Sweden, and occupied and annexed vast tracts of Swedish territory, which in his view remained Sweden. He ranted on and on, about how all Swedes hated Russians, how, after twenty years in Canada it was the hated and historical enemy who was once again causing all the trouble. It was amazing, how feelings that had lain dormant for so many years, could resurface in this violent and poisonous way.

His two young teenage children sat spellbound. Their Dad was normally "dour", yet with a humorous ability, and quite pleasant. But the depression had hit him personally, and there was nothing on earth he could do about it but maybe find his scapegoat.

In the next few years, he, like many others would learn to live with it, and would in fact almost accept it as normal, their living standards drastically reduced. But those unaffected by the drought would survive, unlike many homesteads on the plains that would be abandoned over the next few years. It would be a not uncommon sight to see shuttered homes amidst brown and parched earth - desert-like conditions - where families had given up, and trekked north into Alberta. To the Peace River district, on the northern fringe of the limit of the grain-growing area. Where it was still possible to take up a home-stead, a virgin quarter section of land - a hundred and forty acres - for ten dollars. And start again!

So, after a few more weeks I also became another victim of the depression, when Gustav, I'm sure quite genuinely, said, "Sorry, Bill, I can't employ you any more."

This was happening everywhere. Farmers dispensing with their hired labour, with a, "*We will have to manage*" attitude. And so in turn, adding to, or creating the huge army of unemployed. The transients or hobos who were forever "moving on", and would continue to do so for many years to come, as the depression moved inexorably to its nadir.

Adding to the misery of the prairie farmers, the drought persisted, and "dust storms" entered the vocabulary.

I had been feeling homesick. The solitude of farm life was to me at that time unnatural. I needed buildings, houses, people, lights - all those things that make for town life. So when Gustav paid me my wages, twenty dollars, I wasn't unhappy to return to Regina.

My second entry into Canadian farm life at that time was also inauspicious.

II ~ Central Time

The truck driver drove steadily for about two hours through the unending, treeless, snow covered land. Occasionally talking, but mostly a silent journey. My thoughts now engrossed with the immediate future, of getting through the wilderness just ahead.

As we approached the city, the road became metalled, the traffic increased, and there was a straggle of houses set in their own spacious plots, with larger buildings looming ahead.

The driver said his destination was on the east side of town. I said it was Ok by me. I had never been in Winnipeg before, and regardless of where I was put down, I would need to work my way to the south of the town where the massive marshalling yards were.

I knew from hearsay that they were the largest freight yards in Canada, and only the Chicago yards were bigger. Thus making them the second largest in North America.

I jumped down from the truck, thanking the driver. It was about midday as I wended my way towards the south, buying a loaf of bread from a general store, and ate some of it whilst walking through the suburban streets.

Late in the afternoon I found a beer parlour situated quite close to the railroad.

The various provinces had a variety of laws regarding the sale of alcohol. Manitoba was one of these that was quite relaxed in its drinking habits, and had these premises where any adult could buy liquor and drink at the bar. This one was close to the yards, and sure enough was occupied mostly by railroad workers. I bought a beer with some of my diminishing small change, and attached myself to a group of rail men. After the usual small talk I learned that a transcontinental freight regularly pulled out to the east at two o'clock every morning, and that although I was crazy thinking of riding on top at this time of year, there were seldom any police around in December; because at ten below zero there was nobody stupid enough to hang around. Except for railway workers who had no option.

I stayed in the parlour amongst good company as long as I could.

About midnight, I made my way towards the sound of trains, jostling and juddering as the box cars and assorted trucks were shunted back and forth, slowly assembling a freight train of great length. There were acres of rails ahead and around me. Lines of carriages, box cars, flat cars and dead engines, and railway vehicles of every description.

And of course I became careless! Working my way along these lines of sleeping vehicles, gradually nearing the two locomotives that were very much alive, fussily working back and forth, a number of flat cars, then box cars, cattle trucks and so on, gaining length all the while.

I was at a comfortable distance, watching. Standing now by a dead engine. And it was in that one fleeting moment when I was sure I was the only person around, that these two fur-hatted and belted, big men appeared, apparently from nowhere and accosted me: "Where y' heading, buddy?" as they ran a flashlight up and down me.

In the back of my mind was the dim realisation that these were "Mounties", not railway cops, but they held my future in their hands whichever they were. I was trespassing on railroad property, I was a vagrant, and if they frisked me and found my hundred dollar roll of notes, that would only prove that I had the means to pay my way.

I did literally freeze, but boldly said, "London, England", and awaited their response.

They appeared nonplussed, and looked at each other as if figuratively scratching their heads and thinking, "What do we do with this one?", then said,

"You mean London, Ontario." "No, London, England. There's money awaiting me in Montreal for my passage."

A long silence. Then, "It's ten below zero now, you'll freeze to death up there", pointing to the top of the box cars.

"I'll take my chances", I replied, beginning to sense my luck might be holding.

The flashlight was still wandering up and down me. A long hesitation. Then one of them quickly said, "Look, son, there's cattle on that train, and a cattleman's caboose at the back. They'll probably let you in. Good luck." They then turned and walked briskly away.

I just stood, rooted to the spot, relief flooding over me. Now I was almost cocky. I could jump this one with impunity. I felt I could come out into the open, as if I had been given a ticket to ride. However, commonsense prevailed. I wasn't aboard yet, so I continued to watch, half hidden, until a little later when the shunting ceased. The inevitable pause. Then that melancholic mournful wail, that as ever heralded departure. A sound that could only ever evoke the call of the wilderness; and when heard from a distance could sound like the eerie howl of the coyote, creating the illusion of lost spirits in limbo.

At first I walked alongside, as the train, juddering at first, pulled away. I started trotting as the length of the train began to pass me at a quicker pace; at last the end of the train drew near. The caboose! Don't think, grab a rail and jump. I was aboard.

Puffing with excitement I climbed the first few steps, to the little verandah at the back, and pounded on the back door.

A few moments, voices behind the door. The door was opened and a voice said, "Who are you?" I explained as briefly as I could and then asked, "Are you the cattlemen?" "Sure, come in, shut the door and keep the cold out." The interior was like a cosy small room, with two bunks on each side, one above the other, a small table and chairs. And by far, the most important piece of equipment, a round, glowing wood burning stove in the middle, with a blackened coffee pot simmering on the top.

A haven of comfort and warmth…

"I'm Bob", said the man who had just let me in. "You're lucky, there's a spare bunk." Then he went on to introduce me to the other two cattlemen. "Oh, before you bunk down, in the morning when we feed and water the cattle you can help us, and anybody asks any questions, you're one of us." Then as an afterthought, "Help yourself to coffee."

Bob went on to explain that they were going with the cattle to Toronto, and that when we arrived at Sudbury the train would be divided; they would continue south, whereas I would need to transfer to the other half going east to Ottawa and Montreal.

As Sudbury was almost a thousand miles away through the wilderness I wasn't going to worry about that at present.

The cattlemen were farm hands who had managed to get temporary jobs, shunting cattle across the country. It paid very little but was a comfortable way of travelling, and was little work. Once a day the cattle would be offloaded into corrals, fed and watered, roughly checked to see none were sick, then driven back onto the train.

The rest of the time would be spent reading, smoking, but mostly playing cards and sleeping. They had immediately asked me to join their card game; I had no inclination, and as far as they were concerned, no money. They would probably play all night. I just wanted to get my boots off, climb onto that straw filled mattress on the bunk and sleep.

***

The previous year I had heard about men working their way back to the "Old Country" on cattle ships. There was quite a reverse emigration going on. Disillusioned immigrants seeking to return to Britain, but not having the wherewithal for the fare, tried to get work on cattle ships in lieu of passage money.

I myself had written to two of the shipping companies, offering my services as a cattleman free! For the voyage across the Atlantic. Surprisingly I had received a reply, regretting that they were inundated with similar requests; that they had a waiting list a yard long, and sorry, but there was no point in adding more names to it. I was disappointed but not surprised.

I mused idly as I climbed into my bunk, that twenty-four hours earlier I was sleeping in a little hotel in Corberry. And Frank! Yes, I would always cherish thoughts of that pipe smoking Samaritan. The man who wished me "Good luck" and really meant it.

And also, I mused, that nearly five years before I had been going in the opposite direction, most likely on the same tracks. Then further back... to seeing that small advertisement in the daily paper, "British boys wanted for work in the Dominions. Ages sixteen to twenty years, passage paid, work found." I had shown it to my friend Eric, and had enthused over the possibility of seeing another country. It was different, romantic.

Travelling abroad was an exotic idea, visualised in dreams, and certainly not possible for ordinary working class people. Wealthy people travelled. But our dreams invariably ended with a few days by the sea, which wasn't far away anyhow. And the thrill of reading about other people's adventures, poring over an atlas, fantasizing!

Eric was not impressed. He had his comfortable office job and had no desire to change anything.

I had already decided that Australia and New Zealand were out, too far away; one could not imagine ever being able to return from such a great distance. Whereas Canada, though also a long way away, was not impossibly remote. I answered the advert, and eventually had an interview at Canada

House, in Trafalgar Square.

My parents had done their best to dissuade me, but had not refused. They had to write a letter, granting their permission.

Armed with their letter I kept the appointment.

The interview was perfunctory. A few simple questions, and on my behalf a few equally simple answers. Admittedly, they weren't looking for intellectual types to work on Canadian farms, but I had expected a little more depth. However, I was then directed to another part of the building for a medical examination, which appeared as superficial as the original interview had been. I returned to the first interviewer, to be told that I had been accepted, and would be hearing from them within the next two weeks regarding my ship's passage and times of sailing.

I returned home, outwardly proud, but inwardly quaking at what I had committed myself to.

The romanticism of sailing thousands of miles to a new unknown country, leaving home, family and friends, brought on many a cold sweat and nearly died overnight.

But everybody seemed to be "Oohing and Aahing" at such a bold venture, and of course I wallowed in it. I quite enjoyed the limelight, which in fact had the tendency to suppress any misgivings.

The doubts recurred two weeks later, when a letter arrived from Canada House, stating that I would be sailing on the SS Letitia, from Liverpool, on May 3rd. I had to reply, confirming my acceptance.

I suppose the finality of that letter smoothed away any thought of backing out now. In two weeks I would be "on my way".

Only a catastrophe could intervene now.

Dad was also going to make the most of it. He had never been further than fifty miles from London in his life.

He said, "I'll come to Liverpool and see you off, then go on to Glasgow and spend a week with brother Ernest". One evening a few days later he said, "I don't know how to say this" then hesitated, "but there's a disease called V.D. and I should warn you about it. Do you know anything about it?"

"Oh yes", I replied cheekily, "I've read all about it in your encyclopedia, there's three different kinds."

"What do you mean? I'm talking about a disease called V.D.", he repeated, but he was obviously nonplussed.

He had recently purchased a second-hand set of ten volumes of Harmnsworth Encyclopedia, and I, being at that time an avid reader of anything and everything, had devoured all the unspeakable bits, and immediately thought I knew it all.

Dad, true to his generation, knew that venereal disease could not be discussed - it was a taboo subject - but that it was something to be very scared of. And at this late stage was trying to protect me, to warn me of a danger he thought I was totally unaware of.

I had worked for two years in a piano factory, my initiation was thorough. Life in a large factory was hard, coarse and vulgar, with sexual innuendo rampant. It was a hard school, and sexual exploits and variations were to the forefront of the curriculum and impressed firmly on one.

But Dad just said, "Oh well, Bill, look after yourself." Then I felt silly and put in place. I had tried to show off with my little bit of newly acquired knowledge, and wished I hadn't. Dad was after all a good guy; if he ever said "Damn" it would be an event. Nobody swore or was vulgar in our home, and inwardly it always amazed me how at work, every second word was a swear word, and I fell into it. But at home, or outside the factory I never swore, or needed to.

That quiet but persistent, "One does not swear" syndrome, right from earliest experience - my mother was equally anti-swearing - imbued the whole family with a feeling of repugnance against using expletives. It just wasn't done.

I am reminded of an instance, when my elder brother Arthur and I, were off one evening to attend the Boys Brigade. We were nine and ten years old at the time. We had walked to the end of the road, about a quarter of a mile when our way was blocked by a bunch of rowdy teenagers who cuffed and shoved us around, then refused to let us proceed further. So we gave up and ran home.

Dad of course bristled when we told him what had happened. He put his hat on and said, "Come." So in a high state of indignation, the three of us strode menacingly up the road. Three of the group were still there; mild mannered Dad said, "Is that them?" "Yes", we replied.

He then advanced upon the three tall sixteen year olds and began to harangue them - looking up at them, as he was a short man - using damn and bloody so often that we watched open-mouthed, unbelieving. The youths themselves were bellicose at first, but then Dad, comically put up his fists. An amazing sight, this little man protecting his young. We didn't think it funny at the time, but it was effective: they suddenly turned and ran away. And Dad was instantly deflated; he just gruffly said, "You're alright now", left us and turned back home. It had no doubt taken far more out of him than we realised at the time; he was indeed a peaceful man and such a stirring of the emotions must have been traumatic.

A few days before sailing I left my job and then held a nostalgic farewell party. All my friends, and many cousins and relations came to celebrate my coming adventure. The great day advanced remorselessly; there was plenty of activity leading up to it, so suppressing any adverse feelings.

We were to leave the day before sailing, and stay in a hotel in Liverpool overnight. That in itself was an occasion: I had never stayed in a hotel in my life. But the actual day of departure was a sad one, fraught with emotion. My mother was tearful and quiet. She was a very reserved person at all times, never really showing her feelings. So for any of us to see her cry, meant everybody was strained and uncomfortable.

When Dad and I were ready to leave it was a relief, the excitement could reassert itself.

The train journey to Liverpool was uneventful. Dad was not his usual talkative self. We had an evening to spare when we arrived. Dad said, "Let's go to the pictures", which we did. I don't know anything about the programme, we were just killing time.

It was when we returned to the hotel and Dad made some enquiries about the sailing, that we learned that the ship would arrive at Liverpool that night from Glasgow, and would not dock, but anchor in the river, and passengers from here would be taken out to her by tender, in the morning.

Dad had been looking forward to seeing over a Cunard liner, but that was now impossible. And I had savoured the idea of waving down from the deck, romantically, as the big ship pulled away from the dock.

In the morning when we arrived at the harbour to board the tender, the disappointment was somewhat mitigated by finding among the passengers milling about, a number of other lads like myself, a few with parents, and others standing alone, and as I got talking to two of them the departure felt less painful.

We could see the liner standing out on the river; it looked a long way away and not that big. Dad grasped my hand. "Good luck, Bill." I couldn't speak. Quickly I proceeded to, and then up the gangplank.

A few formalities, and very soon this fussy little tender pulled away from the dock. People standing there, Dad amongst them, quickly became small. The last desultory wave and we were fast approaching the side of the ship which now appeared colossal. Like drawing near to a great black cliff.

The tender, which now seemed tiny against this monster, drew close to a door which had been opened just above the water line in the side of the vessel. A gangplank was pushed out from the door to the tender, and in no time we were walking gingerly across it; it was like entering a black cave, with the massive hull towering above, very intimidating, a feeling of great power within that great mass.

The SS Letitia was seventeen thousand tons, quite a big ship, a Cunard liner that plied regularly across the North Atlantic. The journey to Quebec City where we were to disembark was to take seven days. Then there would be a three day train ride more than halfway across Canada, to Regina, which was our final destination.

We were directed through a maze of corridors, there seemed to be doors, turnings, staircases, everywhere. The floor had an undulating motion, quite slight, but no longer *terra firma*. We found the lounge where the purser was sitting at a table; he allotted us a cabin, and after much searching we discovered the correct number.

It was then that I met for the first time my fellow voyagers. A Scottish youth who had boarded in Glasgow and had had a cabin to himself for one night, and now seemed a little resentful at three more occupants invading his privacy. There was a cockney lad with a coarse East End accent, but a smashing companion he turned out to be. Also a Lancashire lad. The three of them were all a year or two older than me.

Bob, the cockney, had been apprenticed as a dental mechanic and came from a large East End family. But the other two were orphans, my first contact with anybody who had no family; they literally had no relatives of any kind that they knew of, and had been brought up in orphanages from as far back as they could remember, but it didn't seem to bother them.

Luckily we all got on well together, as it was a tiny cabin, with barely room for us to stand up at one time in the space between the bunks. The only furnishings was a wash basin on the wall at the opposite end to the door, which folded into the wall when not in use. A pair of bunks, one above the other, on each side, completed the accommodation. There was room under the two lower bunks for our suitcases, but no space for anything else.

We were not bothered.

After getting acquainted with each other we proceeded up onto the deck. By this time we were already under way and nearing the mouth of the estuary; very soon the sea was all around, with just a smudge of coastline behind. But everything was new and exciting, no time yet for nostalgia.

We had been advised of the various times for meals. There were two sittings for each meal, and everybody had a particular place at a set table at a precise time. We four had been allocated a table together, and a late lunch was our first meal on board. We adjourned to the dining room, another great new experience, a large restaurant crowded with waiters darting about in all directions. We found our table, the waiter presented us with menus. We had a choice! We revelled in the sheer luxury of it all, though it was only third or tourist class as it was called then. We certainly enjoyed our first meal aboard, and as hungry teenagers looked forward to all the other meals to follow.

We found the main lounge, where, when not on deck we would be spending most of the next seven days. It was very large, with a games section at one end where table tennis and board games were played, a reading and writing area, and the main area scattered with comfortable armchairs and small tables. There was a large screen at one end where films were shown every other evening.

The newness and novelty of everything was overwhelming.

Later on as the evening waned, we went on deck and quietly watched the rugged coastline of Northern Ireland slide slowly by, and knew that that was the last sight of the "Old Country" we would have. The next land would be Canada. We didn't talk much then, we were taking a big step and the realisation was now striking home.

We were soon out in the open sea, or the ocean now, as Ireland disappeared as a black line behind us, and the roll of the ship was a little more pronounced, not unpleasantly so; in fact we were enjoying the new sensation of walking towards the bow of the ship, nearly running as it dipped, then climbing uphill as it rose.

The ship was still enormous to us as we explored the two decks we were allowed to use. An upper deck was first class only and we were not admitted to that. We wandered all over the ship, getting to know it and each other.

Late in the evening we retired to our bunks, laughing at the gentle rocking, an agreeable sensation of being lulled to sleep; awakening in the morning to an alarm call on the door at seven thirty. Ours was to be the first serving of breakfast at eight o'clock. I had a peculiar muzzy feeling as my

51

feet made contact with the floor. Then suddenly, a dive towards the basin, and it seemed everything I had ever eaten came up. I vomited agonisingly, I felt ill - so ill, and just wanted to crawl back to my bunk.

"Oh, why did I want to leave home!"

We had been warned the previous day when boarding, about seasickness, and had been advised against going back to bed. The more one fought it and kept active, the quicker one would get their sea legs, and so adapt to the motion for the remainder of the voyage.

Three of us, Cockney Bob, Scotty - the Glasgow lad had immediately become Scotty - and myself experienced similar symptoms and nausea, and sat disconsolately at the sides of our bunks. But Harry, the Lancashire lad was inconsolable. He had vomited and climbed straight back into his bunk. All he would say was, "Leave me alone, I'm ill, leave me alone."

We left him, having decided we had to do something, and cautiously, gingerly, we made our slow way to the dining room. We arrived, gratified at seeing how few had made it and noting how a quietness hung over the meagre few.

Only the steward was as brisk as ever, and had a huge grin spread over his face as he said, "No menus this morning, boys?" We had some tea.

The steward said, "Don't worry about Harry, some take longer than others to get over it, he will be alright."

Back on deck the sun was shining. The ship was still pitching gently, deceptively. A cool breeze felt good, and it seemed most of the passengers on the ship were on deck, suffering various degrees of nausea, many still hanging over the rails. Others were walking sharply round and round the ship, the horribly determined types who would not let a little thing like seasickness get the better of them, and the same ones who told everybody else what to do. "Buck up", "Get moving".

We three sat somewhat dejectedly on a seat, as near midships as possible, trying to ignore that continuous and monotonous up and down, up and down motion of both the vessel and our stomachs. We knew it would pass, one day, maybe two days. But the present held no promise. We were not happy. And the motion of the sea that was so harmless yesterday, we now hated.

Two days later, the large majority of passengers had adapted and fallen in line with the ship's routine. The weather remained spring-like and calm, there was nothing except this vast expanse of empty ocean.

Unexpectedly, porpoises did occasionally dive out of a wave, across a trough and into a following wave, keeping this up alongside of us, causing interest for a time; otherwise we felt completely alone.

The games room, the tennis and the board games, and on deck the game of quoits, were in constant use. Life became very pleasant.

On the third day Harry crawled out of his bunk, looking weak and very much the invalid. Still terribly depressed and non-committal. Our steward had taken him tea and drinks the first two days but he had eaten nothing. Now he managed a little lunch, then we played some rummy in the lounge and walked a number of times round the deck.

It was on the third day that it started raining, and it poured steadily all the next day, restricting our activity as we had spent considerable time wandering around outside. It was now cold, grey weather, reminiscent of any English spring day and equally as distasteful!

Each morning when we went for breakfast, the large clock on the wall of the dining room had been reset, to show those who had watches to readjust them, generally putting them back half an hour or forty minutes, depending on how many knots we had covered the previous day. The distance figure, in miles, being displayed above the clock.

During the night of the fourth day we were awakened by a terrific pitching and tossing, and the next day arose in the morning to a gigantic roaring storm. The liner was rising and falling like the car of a switch back railway, and all the doors leading to the decks had been securely locked. We could only watch, fascinated, through the windows of the lounge which faced the bow of the ship, as wave after enormous wave crashed over us and appeared to bury the vessel, then it reared its massive bow aloft, and seemed to shake the water off like a dog, before plunging into the next wave to repeat the exercise. To walk the interior passages and corridors was like walking up and down a seesaw, that then suddenly plunges down. Having gained our sea legs it became great fun to almost run, then find you are trying to climb the side of a mountain.

We had no sense of fear, enthralled as we were by the size and power of "our" Cunarder. The storm was outside, and we were invincible. However the thought of breakfast did not appeal, we were not nauseous, but a feeling of queasiness was there; one felt it could easily be triggered off by food. But by lunchtime, although the storm showed no signs of abating, we were hungry and went to the half-filled dining room and had a meal.

By the next morning the storm was subsiding and even Harry, who had again taken to his bunk the previous day, decided, with the rest of us, that we needed breakfast.

The dining room clock, and the mileage meter, showed how we had been slowed down by the storm. But later in the day the deck doors were opened, and passengers streamed out to take the fresh air. The wind had died but the swell was still very heavy.

The remaining days passed swiftly, we got acquainted with the rest of our group, and discovered there was a dozen of us all going out under the same scheme. I also found I was the youngest, all the others being eighteen or twenty.

On the sixth day, suddenly there was a cry of "Land!". We had of course been watching for it, seeing who would spot it first, and there it was, a black smudge on the north horizon. We were entering the "Gulf of the St Lawrence", and Anticosti Island was the dark shadow in the distance. A long, low and apparently barren island, which did not alter for many hours as we sailed by.

Everybody was watching pensively, our first sight of Canada, not much conversation. Just a feeling, brought home to us of how far away old

England now was, a gnawing possibility of homesickness, maybe a little fear of the sheer size of the country we were entering.

The ship had quickly become our home. Tomorrow we would be docking in Quebec City and the last phase of our travels would begin. Maybe events were moving too quickly. I wanted to say, "Pause awhile, stop, let me adjust."

The next morning when we went on deck there was a complete change: river banks on both sides, they seemed quite close, compared to the ocean we had just left, and we knew that within an hour we would have arrived at our first destination; leaving our cabin for the last time, saying our goodbyes to many newly made friends, especially our steward who had adopted us as "his boys".

The excitement of disembarkation, the novelty of once again being on firm ground, no longer the up and down motion. The melee of getting the luggage from the hold. Being loaded into a bus and driven to the railway station. No time to see the city, just an instant impression of buildings rising steeply from the harbour, hilly, a closely packed and jumbled look, no time for nostalgia, hurriedly we arrived at the station to board this monster of a train. We did have time to walk to the front of our train and have photos taken beside this hissing giant of a locomotive before we boarded. As the platform was at ground level, we had to climb a few steps up to the carriage doors, which greatly added to the feeling of great size.

When we were aboard and inside, the feeling of size was accentuated by the spacious layout. A wide central corridor meant one could walk the whole length of the train. The seating was arranged in fours, two facing two, with a folding table in between which folded against the wall beneath the window, when it was time to sleep at night. When it was time, the seats were drawn towards each other forming a bed for two persons. A contraption like a huge locker overhead drew down over each of our seats, forming another bed for two, so all passengers had beds, with one blanket and a thin folding mattress. When it was bedtime, we would remove our shoes but not much else, and try to sleep with the continuous *clackety-clack-clackety-click* of the wheels, making it very difficult.

And so, we had a new home for the next three days and three nights it would take to cover the two thousand miles - two thirds of the way across Canada - to our destination at Regina, in Saskatchewan, almost in the middle of the prairies. A city very few of us had heard of before leaving England.

From there we would be found work on farms in the province, and our new life would begin.

For the beginning of the journey the scenery was similar to English spring time countryside. Small farms, irregular fields and many trees. But by the next day we were travelling through Northern Ontario, unbelievable virgin forest and rock outcrop, continuous for hours on end. Occasionally an area had been cleared and a small cluster of houses had been built around a railway station, generally with a large name prominently displayed, as if to justify its existence, for, except for the railway, they had no reason to exist.

The weather did make a difference. The sun shone all day which mitigated against the monotony, and when we had got so used to trees and rocks that we thought they would go on forever, almost suddenly, the view changed dramatically, the trees thinned out - scrubland - then we were entering Manitoba and the prairies. A huge flat open expanse.

Although farmsteads were few and far between, the farmhouses with barns and outhouses stood starkly naked in the flat openness; rarely, a tree belt had been planted, but they also looked out of place, alien in this immensity of space, and insignificant, silhouetted against that magnificent blue sky.

We drank in the picture of these great square fields, laid out like chess boards, very much developed. Square mile after square mile of newly planted cereals, a few inches into growth, giving the effect of limitless lawns.

Then the grain elevators, those colossal red sentinels denoting each small town and seen from many miles away.

There was always a gathering of people watching the train

approach - bell ringing, hooter wailing its banshee song of the plains - the event of the day.

The locals watched, as travellers coming from many distant places, going to unknown destinations, were glimpsed for a few minutes, and no doubt speculated on, and were gone. Trains were infrequent, it was spring and the land responded with its eternal renewing. And the people casually, but intently, watching the trains go by were all part of the scene.

This was a memory that would be captured, and would be stored forever in my mind.

We arrived in Winnipeg, the capital of Manitoba, and the largest Canadian city on our route. Lots of houses and buildings of all kinds. The first time since leaving home we had seen so many. Not crowded together and old, but liberally spaced apart, which we soon realised typified the difference between the two countries. Everything had a new and unsubstantial look. Brick, solid brick, we were used to, but here wood predominated, and somehow it seemed to lack the solidity of our old packed together little brick houses.

The next day we arrived in Regina, ten days from leaving home. We were bussed out to a hostel five miles out of town. Now, each day, one or other of us would be sent out to a farm, farewells would be said, and mostly we would not see each other again. Some kept in touch by post, so over a period we learnt of various incidents. This was 1930, the beginning of The Great Depression, and within a short time it would be shaping most of our lives.

***

57

And now, as I dropped off to sleep, the wheels really did hum a song, and the words of that popular old railroad song wafted through my semi-consciousness.

> *"The wheels hummed a song,*
> *As the train rolled along,*
> *And the black smoke came pouring from its stack,*
> *And the headlights agleam."*

"Coming back, coming back", the wheels rumbled as I drifted towards sleep.

To sleep *and* travel was by far the best way of eating up the miles. And through the wilderness we were now entering, there was little likelihood of rail cops or mounties being concerned with this particular train, or for that matter, this lone traveller. Once again, I was "on my way".

I was being shaken. I surfaced out of a deep sleep. "Come on, Bud", the cattleman was saying, "we're stopping". It was daylight, there was a great bustle of activity as the train juddered to a halt. Suddenly there was a great hurry everywhere. Space had been cleared alongside the track from the surrounding forest, and corrals built. The cattlemen carried loose wattle fences, forming a long fenced corridor from cattle truck to corral. From each wagon the cattle were driven down a ramp, and so to the corral, where the hay and water were already awaiting them. Six separate enclosures to six cattle trucks. It took nearly an hour by the time they were all eating, and everything was done at speed.

Whilst way up ahead, the train crew were supervising the loading of coal and water, beside the huge water tank. Shortly afterwards they had to be driven back, but in the pause between I noticed there were two or three buildings in a clearing beyond the tracks. I trotted over. Sure enough, *"General Store"*, greeted me on one of the buildings. My stomach felt hollow I was so hungry. A loaf of bread, ten cents, a few apples, five cents, and I was on my way back towards the train, thankful that I could eat today.

Bread is absolutely delicious when one is really hungry. The cattle trucks and caboose were at the rear of the train, and the engine, way up ahead, was out of sight. I paused, away from the track, when I saw a guard walk towards the rear of the train. He spoke to the men who were now reloading the cattle, and waited until they were all shut in and doors secured, wattle fences stacked away. Then he returned to the engine crew who were now ready to go. And I returned to the caboose, listening once again for the wail, so evocative of the wilderness, of the hooter proclaiming our departure.

The whole of that day was spent travelling through the monotonous terrain, that I remembered so well, when nearly five years before I had been going in the opposite direction. It was winter now, whereas it had been spring then. But this part of the world was unlikely to change, maybe a haven for the hunter or logger, but even they would have difficulty amongst all this rock.

Hour after hour we chugged through the virtually uninhabited land; a number of times we stopped, and amidst a lot of shunting, various cars or trucks were attached or detached in sidings, then the journey resumed. Throughout the day the cattlemen played cards silently, drank coffee, or lay idly in their bunks. The most taciturn bunch of men to travel with. Men of a few words, was an enormous understatement.

When night came again, it was a relief to stretch out and try to sleep just to relieve the monotony. With so much inactivity sleep did not come easily, and over the steady "*rat a tat tat*" of the wheels, I thought I heard a coyote let out a long mournful howl. A deeply moving sound, fitting to my sense of isolation, sending a shiver down my spine. Though harmless to humans, shy, and actually seldom seen at close quarters, this oft maligned animal had the power, on a still night, as I drifted to sleep, the power to put fear into one.

***

59

It was late March 1931. I had spent the entire winter with Karl in Regina, and had now decided to try farming again.

I had that day, arrived at this large brick farmhouse. Hired out at twelve and a half dollars a month and all found. This was by far the biggest farmhouse I had seen, a massive square red brick house, with veranda at one side, basement, two floors and an attic. The attic was mine, and it was there that I had heard the coyotes calling on that first night. Like a banshee, maybe an omen of what might be in the future.

Mr. Bruce had met me at Tuxford station, about eighty miles west of Regina. "Call me Bob", was the first thing he said, and for all that summer I could not do so. He was old enough to be my father, was below medium height, but nearly as broad, and he looked as strong as an ox. But "Mr. Bruce" he remained, as I hadn't been brought up to call adults by their christian names, let alone a grey haired man in his fifties.

He had a wagon on sleds, and a team of horses. We had driven the fifteen miles to his farm through the flat snow covered prairie. It was still freezing. Bob was uncommunicative and the landscape uninteresting. But very soon this huge house stood out against its bleak surroundings; it was overshadowed by a one hundred foot long barn, stone-built up to ten feet, surmounted by a wooden superstructure, and rising fifty feet above the ground, but standing away from the house across a hundred feet of farmyard, a magnificent building!

Also I noticed as we drew near, that there were power lines radiating from a small outbuilding to house and barn. I soon learned that was where the generator was installed. I was amazed, never having heard of anybody producing their own electricity.

But I soon discovered that once we were in view of his home Bob became almost garrulous regarding his possessions. He had over a thousand acres of land, and in the house all the modern conveniences possible. Even a flush toilet in the basement, but unfortunately the men did not use it. "Men went out to the barn when nature called", said Bob. The toilet was for the exclusive use of Mrs. Bruce, and their teenage daughter, Kate.

When we had arrived and unharnessed the horses, I was introduced to Stuart, Bob's son, who was two years older than me. Then to his wife and daughter. I ate with the family, had the use of a large living room, and had my bed in the attic.

It was a very quiet home, work predominated; maybe, rarely, Bob would be reading a paper in the evening. There were no books anywhere, and Mrs. Bruce would be interminably knitting. They had an attractive modern wireless, which might be switched on for news or weather forecast, but would equally quickly be turned off again. Meals were large but taken in silence, they were purely functional. Once everybody was finished eating we left the table without a dozen words having been spoken amongst the five of us during the meal. I could suddenly have said, "Say, what do you all think of this bloke Hitler?" But of course I couldn't. I hadn't the nerve, and I am sure that all I would have got in response would be four frozen faces, looking at me in disbelief.

I was always ravenously hungry, and was really more concerned with appeasing my demanding stomach than in being involved in conversation. Like on all Canadian farms, there were three meals a day. Six thirty a.m. breakfast, twelve thirty lunch, and supper at six thirty. All meals equally big.

In a few weeks' time when land work would be underway the routine would not vary. For six days of the week, we would rise at five o'clock, feed and harness horses, milk cows, feed pigs, then into breakfast. Out by seven, field work till twelve o'clock, into dinner. Out by one o'clock, field work till six, then into supper. Unharness horses, milk cows, do any other chores and finish about eight o'clock.

One soon fell into the routine, though for a long time it was the lengthy gap between meals that I found most distressing. Back in the "Old Country", there was always lunch mid morning, and tea time in the afternoon. Now it was coffee all the time and nothing between meals.

And anyhow, I had never had to get up at such an unearthly hour.

"Five o'clock, Bill". Every morning Bob's head would poke around the door, and he would say just those three words. And then an hour's work before breakfast, though I was already starving.

Curiously though I put on weight and felt strong. It was in fact an extremely healthy way of life, and there was no denying Bob and Stuart's health. They exuded fitness, and if there was some task requiring extra strength, they competed with each other, Stuart determined to be able to do anything his father could.

After the first few days of doing chores and odds and ends Bob asked, "Can you milk?" "No", I replied. "Well, you'll have to learn then", he said. Everybody on farms milked. I had tried a couple of times the first year, but had not persevered, because I did not have to. Now, "You'll have to learn", brooked no refusal. There were eight milking cows on the farm. Black and white Holsteins. Bob and Stuart normally milked them twice a day, whilst I did other chores, grooming and harnessing the horses and feeding the pigs.

The cream was separated from the milk and every other day Bob would take it into town to the creamery, the skimmed milk being used to feed the pigs.

Next morning Bob said, "Have a go at Dolly." She was the oldest and most placid cow. I took the little three legged stool and sat at the right end of the cow then commenced pulling at her teats, as other milkers did. Funny how a cow can immediately recognise a stranger. Instead of continuing eating as all her sisters were doing, she swung her head round and stared unblinking! Her protruding saucer-sized eyes surveying me and making me feel stupidly incompetent. She mooed a little and teetered fretfully on her forelegs, whilst I pushed my head firmly against her flank and tried to grip her long slippery teats, all the while giving that squeezing downward motion, which in theory would issue forth long squirts of creamy milk. I did eventually succeed in producing half a pint of milk. In the meantime all the other cows had been milked!

The base of my thumb ached, it ached like fury! Twice a day. And then gradually as the days passed it did not hurt.

It was weeks before I could finally sit beside a cow and nearly fill a bucket of frothing milk in ten minutes, without my muscles complaining, and with the animal eating or chewing the cud as if I didn't exist. It became a very satisfying feeling; there was a rhythm to the soothing jets of milk converging into that pail, that, at five thirty in the morning was almost hypnotic.

Wake up! She's run dry!

Sunday was a different day. Bob's head would poke around the door. "Six o'clock, Bill". The routine had altered by one hour. All the usual chores before breakfast, but then a considerable difference. The men dressed in suits, the women put their best clothes on. A team of horses was hitched to the large buggy, and off to church.

It was quite a festive occasion, all the carriages and wagons tied to a hitching rail, lots of "Hi-ing" and nodding as we entered the churchyard.

It was a small brick church that had been erected in 1898, when the area was first settled. A large graveyard surrounded it, but no more than a dozen headstones, signifying how recent the settlement of this district had been. It looked in need of corpses, so different to the old cemeteries back home, crowded and old, ancient with centuries of dead bodies.

After the service everybody stood around, rather self consciously in their best clothes, making small conversation, mostly about crops and animals. However this was a regular weekly event. I was introduced to various people, and although I had no interest in religion, I looked forward to this small opportunity of meeting and chatting to others.

Most farms had "hired men", some had "hired girls" also. The church service, like the school dances which were held once a month, were the two regular events that gave us young ones a chance to get together. We did the chores again on Sunday afternoon, and retired early to bed, ready for another week. After a couple of weeks, by the middle of April, Bob said, "We can start field work next week."

63

The snow had gone, the sun shone, and the quick and short prairie spring was upon us. Throughout the winter the frost could well have penetrated four feet into the ground, and would be rising as moisture well into June. But now the topsoil was soft and friable and land work could commence.

Bob had over twenty heavy shire work horses. They had roamed the surrounding prairie throughout the winter, foraging for themselves. Growing fat with long thick coats. Staying together and generally returning home every week or so for the block of salt that was left permanently - or replaced when necessary - in the yard.

One team of horses had been kept in all winter, for general use, and also a riding mare called Pearl.

"Can you ride, Bill?" Bob had asked during my first few days. "Nope", I replied uncomfortably. "You'll have to learn, then", he repeated, again in a tone brooding no question.

"On Sunday we will saddle Pearl, and you can start learning", Bob proclaimed.

So, in great trepidation, for the next few days I spoke soothingly to her, and studied this big slender horse, praying I wasn't going to make a fool of myself, or rather that she wouldn't make a fool of me.

The day arrived too quickly. When Stuart said, "We will saddle Pearl", I was glad Bob wasn't around. I was more at ease with Stuart.

The horse was ready, saddled and bridled and I tried to be nonchalant as I placed my foot in the stirrup. It worked! I was up, but the ground seemed such a long way away. Handing me the reins, Stuart said, "Just walk her, trot a little, keep a tight rein, and don't leave the yard. Ok, when you're ready, carry on."

When I was ready! I *was* ready. Already in a real sweat, but casually I said, "That's Ok, Stuart."

He gave me a doubtful look, but being a nice guy, he walked into the barn and left me. I touched Pearl's flanks with my heels and she walked, and so began my first horse ride.

Later Stuart came out of the barn and said, "You're doing alright, dismount now, unsaddle her, put her in the barn, and so get used to her."

Within a couple of weeks I was enjoying the exhilarating sensation of cantering across the open fields.

Now with the main working season upon us, one morning Bob declared it was time to get the horses home, then told me to saddle up Pearl and round them up.

Steve had phoned and said our horses were near his place; Steve Plunkett was our nearest neighbour, another big farmer. All the farmers for miles around watched the various groups of horses roaming the prairie all winter, and kept each other in touch with their movements.

Bob directed me to Steve's farm five miles south, where he said Steve would point out our horses to me. "Bring them back steady", were my instructions.

I trotted comfortably to the farm. Steve jumped on a horse and accompanied me a further two miles south, and eventually pointed to a bunch of horses half a mile away. "There you are, Bill, they're all yours", then turned and left me.

I rode carefully around these twenty or more heavy horses, and slowly got them into a close bunch, and heading in the right direction. It was a powerful sensation as they all gradually started trotting. They might be heavies, they were also very frisky, and a trot soon became a gallop. Instinctively I didn't think Bob would appreciate twenty or more sweating horses galloping into his yard. So well before the house came into view, I eased up, allowing them to calm down and enter the yard at a decent slow pace. Now there was the tricky job of haltering them. They had had six months of freedom, and were restive and half wild. Bob and Stuart who knew each one by name, slowly walked amongst them, talking gently all the time, then slipping a halter over the head of one and gently walking it towards the barn. Some were rather difficult, but a bucket of oats drawn

65

gently under their noses generally did the trick, and within an hour all were back in the stalls they had vacated the previous fall.

For six months now they would work, only being put out to a small pasture each night. Their liberty was gone. They were hairy, fat and soft. From now on they would be fed with hard grain and hay. Groomed, and very soon they would be sleek and strong, rippling with muscle, the real heavy shire working horse.

After a few days they were harnessed. Some were already docile, but a few of the more spirited ones had an unpleasant tendency to kick, when they felt the harness on their backs.

Another day or two, and eight were harnessed and led into the yard. This was Bob's outfit. When they were hitched together Bob took the reins, four lines spreading over a row of eight horses, and walked them round and round the yard. Stuart and I stood ready, prepared for action, if they should get out of hand. They did not like their new role, this demise of liberty, but Bob's commands were insistent, and soon they settled down. They were then put back in their stalls with harness remaining on them.

Then it was my turn. Bob had said, "Can you drive an outfit?", and this time I could respond in the affirmative. "Yes, five horses", as I had had a little experience the previous year at the Swede's farm. Bob had grunted, and now another six horses were assembled line abreast, and four lines connecting were handed to me. Now it was my turn to manoeuvre the unwilling animals round and round the yard, commanding stops and starts, and right and left, feeling self-conscious at having to raise my voice as Bob and Stuart watched.

However all went well, into the barn they went and tomorrow field work proper would commence.

Stuart drove a tractor. And had been disking for a number of days, ahead of when seeding proper would start. The disk harrows had become a controversial implement. Previously the land had been ploughed regularly, but ploughing, even with three or four furrow ploughs was slow, time-consuming and labour intensive. The black earth of the prairies was very fertile, and the average plains farmer had soon decided that the disks pulled behind an outfit of horses, or a tractor, covered three times the acreage, turned the topsoil to a fine tilth, and the land was immediately ready for seeding.

The implement, the disk harrows, were themselves a series of saucers, each eighteen inches in diameter, making a row twelve or more feet across, depending on the number of individual saucers. The action, when in motion, was to churn the soil over to a depth of five or six inches, as against the turning of a furrow by the share of a plough. Hence, a disk harrow twelve or more feet wide could cover an enormous acreage in one day. This also partly explained why a farm of over a thousand acres could be run by three men. The disks had become a way of prairie farming, but many voices queried the wisdom of these methods, along with the lack of use of any fertilisers.

And drought had raised its ominous head further south the previous year.

Generally, the farmer's only resource in the protection of the fertility of his land, was a three year cycle. Wheat, oats and fallow. A third of the land would be summer fallow, the term most used when the land was unused. During the summer this idle land would be constantly disked and harrowed to create weed growth, and subsequently destroy them. By this method, the land, "the Good Earth", was expected to regain its fruitfulness from the elements and the rest alone.

Again many voices were raised in protest at this prodigal use of the soil, and of the dire consequences that might soon follow.

But the snow, and particularly the rain, came at the right time, the crops were very good, and had been for years.

On a Sunday, when the farming folk gathered for church, they - at this time of year - vied with each other, boasting of how many acres they had seeded, or how many acres they had covered in any one day. They certainly did not discuss farming practices in depth. That was for people who wrote articles in papers, and had no practical knowledge.

On the evening before land work was due to start Bob said, "Before we get the horses out in the morning we will butcher the steer." He had always been called "Old Mac", until a few weeks previously, when he had been castrated, for being "a bit past his prime". He had always been comparatively docile for a bull, and no doubt since that event, any fading interest he had had for cows was gone. And now he was just "the steer". The following morning, after breakfast, the three of us, Bob, Stuart, and myself went out to the barn. Bob, picking up an axe on the way, and walking easily with it, as if off to the wood pile to split some logs. I had never seen an animal killed before, and up to then had no idea of the means of execution. In fact, I had never given thought to how animals were killed, but now I felt instantly queasy. Bob led "Old Mac", unresistingly by the ring in his nose, out into the yard.

Where firstly, one noose was placed around his neck, and the loose end taken by Stuart, who was standing about six feet away to the right. Then the second noose was placed with the first one, the loose end being handed to me, as I stood at an equal distance on the other side. These were merely precautions in case things didn't go quite to plan.

During the preparations, Bob had been talking quietly to Mac, whilst holding the ring in his nose. He continued to murmur as he let go of the ring, and stepped slowly back a yard, now slightly swinging the axe. It seemed a split second as he suddenly swung the axe over his head in a perfect almighty arc, the blunt end landing precisely in the middle of Old Mac's forehead. *Thwack!* Just above the eyes, and the ox collapsing instantly, like an empty sack.

I think it was the skill that Bob showed that flabbergasted me most. That colossal swing, so swift it had taken me as completely by surprise, just as it had poor old Mac. I knew Bob was strong, but that sudden unleashing of power instilled in me a kind of awe, which almost nullified the feeling of facing death for the first time.

The first week of land work saw us settle into a daily routine. Stuart with his tractor and disks. Bob, with his eight horse outfit and seed drill. And I, following with my six horses and spiked harrow to disturb and level the seed bed. I sat on a little metal seat, raised on two wheels, behind the implement. With four lines in my hand, and for mile after mile I followed the wheel line of the seeder. At first I seemed a long way behind my horses, but quickly got used to it.

Half a mile, turn round, half a mile, turn round. The horses adapted speedily to the steady pace, five hours in the morning, five hours in the after noon. Good strong plodders, we followed the seeder, straight as a die, the land lying flat to the horizon in every direction.

In two weeks' time hundreds of acres had been sown, mostly in the warm spring sunshine. There was no rain. But in April it seldom rained, as Bob said, "There's plenty of frost coming up, plenty of moisture in the soil."

Mrs. Bruce was very nice. A quiet grey-haired woman, inarticulate, always working, even in the evenings knitting or sewing. And now, as well as looking after her flock of hens, working for hours in the garden, or as much time as she could spare from all the cooking and housework. She obviously loved growing plants. I remember her saying one day, almost apologetically, "I've been trying to grow roses for years, I'll show you." I was quite surprised when she took me to the south side of the house, and there were a few struggling pathetic bushes. Nursed, covered with straw in the winter, but barely alive. A classic case of the struggle for survival. Standing looking at them she said somewhat wistfully, "You have roses in England. Yes?" but I thought, they're not covered in snow for half a year, nor suffer temperatures of thirty or forty below zero for weeks on end. But she would strive to grow her roses and other unsuitable plants, regardless of the severe climate.

The wheat had all been sown, and now at the end of the first week in May, we had nearly finished sowing the oats. "It will rain soon", said Bob, as the new fresh green growth began to appear. All cereal crops on the prairies grew fast. Planted in April and harvested in August. Only rye could be sown in the fall, grow a little, then survive the heavy frosts and restart into vigorous growth in the spring. Rye was mostly grown by German or mid-European farmers, as the staple of their black bread.

It did *not* rain! Instead it began to blow, heavy leaden skies that should have brought rain, but did not. It was irritating and worrying. Then one night the wind gathered real strength, and roared around the house. The threat in that wind was ominous.

I wasn't sleeping, I doubt if anyone in that house was. There were footsteps below, long before daybreak.

In the morning we could not believe our eyes or our ears. From the house the barn could not be seen, like in an old fashioned London fog, but swirling and roaring ceaselessly. The whole sky was filled with dust, a khaki-brown atmosphere, like the whole firmament was in tumult, dim and sunless.

The three of us pushed our way to the barn, no word had yet been spoken. We stood dumbstruck.

Bob said, "Bill, make your way over to the pasture gate; if the horses are there count them, don't open the gate, then come back." All the horses were crowded together, their backs to the wind, forlorn and silent. I left them.

Bob and Stuart were milking when I got back. With fine dust trickling into my shirt, and my eyes feeling gritty, I fed the pigs at the end of the barn. By which time the milking was finished, and we struggled, fighting the wind, back to the house. Everywhere being covered by a very fine dust.

Breakfast was taken in stolid silence, as if nobody dared voice their feelings. A catastrophe was happening they couldn't believe. So! Carry on as usual.

When breakfast was finished Bob said, "Leave the horses where they are, nothing we can do till the wind dies", and left the table abruptly.

The wind did not die. All that day it raged like some tormented spirit. It roared, and taunted man's puny efforts against this colossus. We dithered around and waited helplessly. Mrs. Bruce and Kate, against all common sense, started sweeping and cleaning, but silently.

Understandably, one fights, one is not defeated.

Stuart and I went off to the barn, walking up and down, looking out of a window, disbelieving. An odd word, but what was there to say, it was too awful to discuss. That accursed wind must ease up sometime. Occasionally we caught sight of Bob wandering about, forcing himself against the wind. No doubt, in some futile senseless effort to combat this malignant force.

He did not come in for dinner.

We idled the day away, the wind persisting remorselessly.

I remembered the previous year, my first experience of the Chinook, that hot wind that raced unchecked out of the south west. That, was later in the year and not so violent. The Chinook in winter is a welcome friend, warm and soft. This present mad convulsion of the elements was like doomsday, maybe a judgement!

Bob came in for supper, haggard, dust covered and morose. Nobody broke the silence.

I was tired, with the tiredness of impotence. I went early to bed. During the night I awoke suddenly. The wind was merely whispering: "*wake up, wake up, and see what I have done*", it seemed to murmur. And as dawn broke at four thirty I rose. As had all the members of the family, and went and stood in the living room as daylight spread. Watched in amazed fascination at a view of utter desolation. Where, two days before the prairie had extended like a huge lawn to the horizon, with new crops three or four inches high, and a brilliant fresh green. Now, through the still murky air, it was brown and lifeless. Not a living thing, as if a slate had been wiped clean. The yard, the buildings were covered with an inch of dust, so fine it rose like smoke as one walked.

Each farm had a road allowance around its boundaries. Every mile North South, and every two miles East West. These were dirt roads that had been graded to raise the surface, and ditches were thus formed on each side. They invariably had a two strand barbed wire fence alongside. The Russian thistle - tumble weed - when ripe and dry, rolled across the plains and was trapped by the barbed wire. A common sight everywhere, fences clogged with this tenacious weed. And now the fences had become dirt walls, and in fact in many places, the mounds that had been fences, were now the only evidence of where the roads had been. All the ditches had been levelled, and if one stepped where they had been, one sank a foot or more in fine dust.

There was the odd corner, a small verdant patch, that had for some inexplicable reason, survived. But in effect the whole hundreds of acres of grain had gone, and tons of topsoil with it.

A few days to adapt and accept the inevitable.

A heavy shower of rain and Bob bounced back, "It *must* really rain soon, I'll re-sow; it's too late for wheat, but maybe we will get a crop of oats."

Once again out on the seemingly fallow land, we disked, and seeded, and harrowed for a week.

The weather was unkind, it was very hot, heavy clouds did rarely roll over but it still did not rain, and the wind was threatening all the time.

Bob had become dishearten and fatalistic, almost sensing he was losing the fight. And sure enough, in the middle of June, the wind again gathered its strength and created another huge dust storm. This time during daylight. We watched resignedly, Bob, Stuart and I, grouped together, as gigantic black billowing clouds rolled towards us from the distant horizon. Like spectators at an event beyond one's comprehension. The difference being that we all had now surrendered to the inevitable, as millions of tons of topsoil - beautiful, fertile, black earth - approached, in the form of a massive dust storm.

Like a picture on a screen in slow motion.

The wind increasing ahead of somebody else's airborne dried soil, very soon bearing down upon us, once again recreating that inferno of choking dust. Laying waste to our second attempt at producing a crop.

Within a few hours it had gone, and so had Bob's second sowing of grain.

Most of the whole area of the southern prairies had suffered the same fate, hundreds of square miles had been renamed the "Dust Bowl";

everywhere had an arid appearance, dry and brown.

This was to be the great drought of the thirties. The worst in North American history, when billions of tons of topsoil were blown off the over cultivated, and over-grazed earth, and darkened the sky over eastern cities at noon. And it was to last the best part of a decade. It extended from Kansas and the mid-west states of the USA, through the Dakotas and Montana, up into the prairie provinces of Canada; and like the great economic depression, lasted almost throughout the thirties, and would soon be coining another phrase, "The Dirty Thirties".

Shortly after the second "blow", Bob said, "Bill, I'll have to let you go, no crop, no money."

I had heard it before, one didn't get the sack or the bullet, one was "let go". But Bob did say, "unless you want to stay the summer for your board", adding, "There's a government scheme being raised, I'll find out about it."

The onset of The Great Depression the previous year, along with the drought and dust bowl of this year, had quickly given rise to an army of unemployed, the hobos or transients. A moving mass of men, wandering, seeking work, and "bumming" to live. Begging was not a word used! Somehow bumming was less obnoxious.

The provincial prairie governments introduced a scheme, whereby any farmer who retained his hired help was paid five dollars a month, and his help was paid the same. This was an effort to control the floating mass of labour, which was speedily threatening to clog the larger towns and small prairie cities.

Even in 1931 the statistics were frightening: a quarter of the labour force of the country was without work, and the depression deepening all the time. There were lines of hopeless men queuing patiently at soup kitchens which had been set up in all large towns. Time - they had plenty! And the freight trains, with their abundance of poker-faced passengers seated on the roof, was ample testimony to the amount of wasted labour travelling vaguely about the country, in search of non-existent jobs.

Bob filled in the necessary papers, and I stayed on.

The routine had been swept away. Normally, field work would continue throughout the summer, working the fallow land till harvest began.

Some rain did fall, but meagrely.

The land gradually became covered with a crop of weeds, and in late summer the earth was green again, but only with unwanted growth which the farmers watched mature, but dared not till. The idea being, to turn it in just before it ripened to try and replace some fibre in the soil, and so prevent it blowing again.

There was an enormous amount of criticism at the time, of the farmers who, it was suggested, had brought disaster upon themselves, by greed. Robbing the good earth and giving nothing back. Now suddenly they were all seeking alternative methods. Strip farming, whereby strips of land were planted with grass and alternate strips with cereals; or planting rye in the fall, to gain good root hold before the spring. Or tree belts. All of which had been suggested many many times before, by people with foresight. But really it did not relate to the present.

Bob at least could weather it out. His was not a poor homesteading family. His forebears might be Scottish, but they had farmed for many generations in Ontario. He had sold up and moved out twenty years before, and purchased a two section farm. He built his red brick house and stone barn, and generally had been a successful and prosperous farmer. Crops had been good, bad, or indifferent, but always there were crops. Up to this year. Nothing comparable to this had ever happened before.

There were many schemes introduced in an attempt to alleviate the hardship. The land taxes that many farmers could no longer pay, were often worked off in road making. Under one of these provincial government operations I was employed with a team of horses and a grader, at resurfacing some of the dirt roads in our vicinity. Of course I was working for Bob, and he was using me to clear some of his commitments, and keep me occupied.

But although we still worked a ten hour day, I enjoyed the work, as there were many hired men in the gang; we worked close together, and the atmosphere was very convivial.

Bob had one big advantage over most of the other farmers in this part of Saskatchewan. A half mile north of his farm the land obliquely dropped away, and fifty feet below the normal level of the plain was a lake. The name of which was evocative of what "had" been. "Last Buffalo lake" was twelve miles long and about half a mile wide. A long narrow slit in the prairie, which stretched endlessly from it in all directions.

It was virgin, quite desolate and isolated, used only by migrating birds of every description.

I remember one Sunday in spring. I had wandered down to the lakeside, as I often did, fascinated by the wilderness, and was amazed at seeing the whole surface of water covered in swans. I persuaded Stuart to come and see, what he wouldn't believe I had seen. And for an hour we gazed in wonderment at thousands upon thousands of elegant white swans resting and eating, one step nearer their nesting grounds much further north.

The next day they were gone, the lake returning to its virginity.

Bob had a half section of land running north to the lake. This was made up mostly by a long irregular ravine, sloping away from the farm to the water's edge, the lake forming the northern boundary. There were areas of rough grass, but mostly scrub bushes and small willows. Anything big or useful had already been cut and used for fence posts. There were many impenetrable jungle-like tracts.

Twice that spring the ravine became a hunting ground. One day a sow, whose gestation period was up, broke out of the yard and disappeared into the ravine. We searched for days without success. But ten days later she came grunting back into the yard with a dozen piglets, milling and squealing around her, and as much to say, "I can look after myself, look what I've brought back."

The second incident was very different. One of Bob's mares was due to foal. He had kept her in the barn, as he had had trouble when she foaled before. How she got out, nobody knew. But we searched the ravine till dark, and started again the next morning. Later in the day Bob did find her, she was half way through foaling and dead.

One of my chores during that summer was feeding and looking after the twenty pigs being fattened for the fall market. Like all animals, there were some awkward ones.

Mostly, when I approached the sty with my two buckets of swill and barley, they were raising the roof with their squealing, and milling around the feed trough. But a particular one had the habit of jumping up over the trough and trying to get the food before I could tip it. He was so aggressive I began to get annoyed at his persistence. So one Sunday morning I decided to teach him a lesson. I perched the feed pail on top of the fence rail, preparatory to tipping. As usual this particular swine jumped over the others in his attempt to be first. I balanced the bucket with my left hand, and punched him on the snout with my right. He was a fraction quicker than me. I missed, instead of his snout my fist caught his jaw; I dislodged a small tooth - which didn't even distract him - but when I drew back I realised I had a pig's tooth firmly embedded against the bone, between the first and second joint of my index finger. Heck! What to do?

I could not bend the finger, it didn't really hurt; I could see a bit of white bone where it had entered, but no way could I get it out, no matter how much I wriggled it about. I was left with a pig's molar, about one and a half inches long, firmly implanted in my finger.

I had to tell Bob, but I couldn't pluck up the courage. I carried on with my chores, the usual routine, went to church, came back, went in at midday and had our meal in the usual silence, and nobody noticed I had a stiff finger.

However, after a mentally agonising afternoon, I realised I had no option.

One of the Canadian Pacific Railway engines I travelled with.

Sunday best, December 1931.

Lipton Farm, 1930-34.

My favourite horse "Lucy". 1932, Regina Town.

Karl the German wood worker.

The Muck's children in winter.

The most comfortabke farm I worked in.

The Barton family, 3rd May 1933.

Setting the plugh teams up, 29th July 1933.

Down on the farm hay making, August 1934.

82

Going home aboard the SS Ausonia on the St. Lawrence river.

Bill Warren, the author in the 1950's.

I located Bob working in the garden. "Mr. Bruce, I punched one of your pigs this morning that had been making a nuisance of itself, and I've got his tooth stuck in my finger." I rattled it out, showing him my hand at the same time.

He felt my finger, almost in disbelief. "Christ! Why didn't you tell me before?"

"Sorry", I said, "I shouldn't have punched him."

"You realise I'll have to cut it out, this should have been seen to long ago. Heck! You're not afraid of me, are you?"

There was no answer to that, he had been so morose and unapproachable since the dust storms that I had avoided him as much as possible. He said, "You know there's no doctors around here, nearest one is in Moose Jaw, sixty miles away. It will hurt, I've only got iodine."

I had visions of showing myself up as he slit my finger - and remembered a very similar episode when I was about eleven.

I had been playing with Dad's tools in the garden shed, and had somehow got a small splinter of wood under the fingernail of my left hand index finger. I couldn't get it out, so tried to ignore it. A few days later the finger began to swell, so I explained to my mother what had happened; she could locate no splinter but bathed it. However, in a couple more days it was so swollen, and my arm aching, that Dad carted me off to the doctor.

Dr. Lamb was a big stout man, white haired, and cycled his way around to his patients. His little surgery was in the parlour of his home; he wore a deaf aid, spoke very loudly, and one thought of him as very old and omnipotent. He was a very well known figure in the locality.

He diagnosed a poisoned finger. "Keep it immersed in near boiling water for two days, then bring him back, father, and I'll lance it."

For two days my finger continued to swell painfully. The fateful morning arrived when Dad said, "We will have to go now." Poor old Dad, I think he was shaking more than me. A glance by the doctor, then very sternly, "Father, take Billy's right hand, hold very tightly, and turn your head

85

away", at the same time, holding my left hand firmly and taking up the lance, then a second later, wow! A searing pain. I yelled the room down as he slit the ball of my finger open, squeezed the finger hard, pus shooting out, then quickly, "Father, press his head between his knees or he will faint". I didn't, and although I was trembling all over, within minutes I was aware that the previous throbbing pain was gone; what a relief!

Bob had produced a small very sharp knife and said, "Hold your wrist with your left hand", whilst he held my finger and sized it up. Then he quickly nicked my finger by about a quarter inch where the tooth had entered. Squeezed hard suddenly, and a long white tooth shot out into his hand. The relief was instant. He almost light-heartedly grinned as he said, "This will be the worst part", laying my finger in iodine, then bandaging it. The next day it was swollen, but within a couple of days that subsided, and it was back to normal.

That particular pig never *did* learn anything, remaining as greedy as ever. But I had learned to be philosophical about *him*, and never attempted to punch a pig's snout again.

It was my eighteenth birthday, a Saturday. I received regular letters, weekly, from my parents, and replied regularly myself. So on the seventeenth, the day before, I received this solitary card from home, and was feeling depressed. It should be a different day, but what on earth could make it different.

"Mr. Bruce, it's my birthday tomorrow, could I go into town for a haircut?" I came out with this at suppertime. He came out of his semi-permanent trance, "Your birthday? Yes, yes, of course", as he came to, "take Pearl, have a day off", he added.

Next morning I saddled Pearl, and trotted happily off to town. "Town" of course was a ridiculous misnomer. Four huge grain elevators overlooked a couple of dozen houses, a small village back home. But there was a post office, general store and a barber. And not forgetting the church.

There were a few cars, people going about their business, activity!

It was a grand feeling to hitch Pearl to the rail in front of the barber's and enter. Even in such a small town the barber had his revolving chair in which you would sit, and he would manoeuvre you up and down and round and round, with a flourish, talking incessantly though that was music to my ears, all the while being very professional. I had had a shock that first year, to have to pay a dollar for a haircut, it seemed so exorbitant when earning so little. But quite an operation was made of it, and it was my birthday!

Many hours later, after wandering about, and chatting to whoever I could, I made my way back to the farm, feeling better and much lighter on my head.

As the summer drew to a close, the lack of any harvest seemed strikingly unnatural. Often Bob would have to stop and think, in an effort to find me chores to keep me employed, and then find me some minor task just to keep me occupied. Normally this would have been the busiest time of year, with everybody working from dawn to dusk.

But not this year.

The silent atmosphere persisted, though I had got used to that. But I gradually thought things out, and decided, enough was enough. It was September, and I needed houses, people, around me. Maybe it was my cockney instincts asserting themselves, whatever it was, one morning I said, "Mr. Bruce, I'm packing up and returning to Regina."

When the day came and I had packed my case, Bob said, "I'll run you into town." The family were all very nice, all of them regretting that I had been with them during such a bad year. And Bob shook my hand tightly, as he wished me luck when we arrived at Tuxford.

With a few dollars left in my pocket, I caught the train for Regina. A light-hearted feeling already, after six months away from town life.

A couple of hours later, when we arrived, this small city suddenly took on the air of a thriving, bustling metropolis. And walking slowly along the streets, looking at buildings and people all around, cars, streetcars, "everything" gave me a marvellous feeling of elation.

I had a coffee and a piece of pie in a café. Then thought, "Whilst I feel like this, I'll go and see my old boss, before something deflates me."

Ten minutes later I found South Railway Street and walked brazenly into the old workshop, still carrying my old suitcase, and still on a "high". Straight into the office with a, "Hi, boss, how are you?" This sharp little Yorkshire man was temporarily lost for words.

Not quite the same, as once, six or seven months back, when he had dramatically appeared from out of his office, unable to speak, and pointing uncontrollably at me and his coat, which was hanging on the door. Something quickly clicked, and I grabbed the atomiser from out of his pocket; he grabbed it. A few seconds and he was breathing normally. Later, gruffly, he told me had asthma. Now, when he had stopped shaking his head in disbelief, he said, "I suppose you want your job back."

I replied, "Sure."

"How was the farm?"

"Lots of dust, not much else."

"Ok", he said, almost resignedly.

"Leave the case with Karl, we will go and meet the folks and have a meal. Jump in the car."

He had said the same thing just a year previously, and *"Meet the folks"* sounded just like home.

III ~ Eastern Time

Once more, I was being shaken. "Wake up, Bud, we're stopping." The train was juddering and clanking slowly to a halt.

Again, all the activity of unloading the cattle, feeding and watering, and driving them back into their trucks; whilst I located a general store and purchased my loaf of bread, and kept my distance until the train was once again in motion.

This morning the scenery had changed yet again, and although we were still in Northern Ontario, gone were the rock and forest. We were through the wilderness, into an older settled part of the province. The farmhouses looking mature and established, with fully developed tree belts around the buildings, smaller, irregular fields with ledges in a gently undulating countryside. Except for the snow it could have been somewhere in England. The temperature had also changed. There was still plenty of snow, it was still freezing, but somehow the prairie iciness had gone; which was some relief to me, as soon I might be riding on top once again.

Sometime during the night we had passed out of the Central Time zone into Eastern Time, gaining another hour on our journey as we headed steadily east.

The cattlemen were more talkative now, as in a few hours' time we would arrive at Sudbury. The train would split into two, they would head south with the cattle for Toronto. And I would once again be left to my own devices, and hopefully catch the other half going towards Ottawa and Montreal. They did warn me, to watch for the cops in the more urbanised areas I would be entering.

The clattering of points, many rails appearing, and odd buildings around, denoted we were coming into Sudbury. This town, quite large, was famous for, and existed only because of nickel. One of the largest nickel producing areas of the world. Its slag heaps were equally infamous, as moonscapes.

This is where, as the train slowed down, I thanked the cattlemen and prepared to leave my comfortable bunk and jump down onto the tracks. I went a little distance from all the shunting and activity, watching the many engines involved and needing to see which locomotive the cattle were with. That would not be the one for me.

·I had seen no other travellers since leaving Calgary - so figured there was nothing for cops to hang around for. However, there were lots of buildings around as we were on the edge of a big town. So my eyes were everywhere, anxious for the trains to get under way, and moving about to keep warm. I needed to start warm as I had a feeling I might have to ride on top, and nearly three hundred miles exposed to this icy weather was a poor prospect.

Within an hour, that melancholy wail of the hooter sounded. To me, standing quite a distance away, that sound always evoked a poignant sense of loneliness. On the other hand it meant "we're leaving", and I watched as the cattle train slowly pulled away.

Shortly afterwards, another forlorn double wail, and a shorter train was moving off. Now I needed to come alive, that was *my* train. Whilst I had been watching the shunting I had seen no empty box cars. But no option now, as I sprinted, measuring my pace alongside the moving train. Watching with a last hope of an open door, but as the end of the train approached, and the train speeded up, I thought, "No luck", as I grabbed a rail and was jerked up and onto the couplings between two cars. I remained standing - shaking a little - where I was, until we were clear of the town. Then climbed the iron rungs, set in the end of each box car, to the top. Then sat on the edge of the walkway, with my back to the engine. What to do?

It would take all day to cover the two hundred and fifty miles to Ottawa. I was hungry. I had eaten the last of my bread, and the cold was really worrying me.

I knew I could not sit there for long, the train was gathering speed, and the chill was quickly penetrating my clothes. The temperature was about ten degrees below freezing, not really cold by Canadian standards. But I *had* to find an empty cattle truck or flat car, somewhere I could curl up, get a blanket round me and survive the day.

I crawled slowly along the top of the train, box car to box car, towards the engine. Every once in a while climbing down between the cars, standing over the couplings, beating my arms about to get warm, then climbing back up and continuing my slow progress forwards. An hour sufficed for me to arrive at the first car of the train, behind the coal tender.

The entire train consisted of locked and loaded cars. By now I was feeling desperate, noting my cheeks and forehead nip, as frostbite attacked; raising my hands to my cheeks and feeling nothing; my ears were protected by the ear flaps of my cap. The tip of my nose no longer had any feeling. I clambered down on to the coal tender, which seemed very long, and still looked to be a great distance from the locomotive.

Now at last, a minor piece of luck.

The coal at the very back of the tender was a foot or more below the top of the parapet of the container, whereas tons of coal were heaped up high in front. Also the smoke and steam was swirling around and above me creating a cocoon of comparative warmth as I settled into a corner, pulling my blanket over and around me, trusting this fog of dirty moisture would keep me unseen from the train driver and fireman.

I rubbed away at the frozen skin of my face and nose until feeling returned. Then slipped into a comatose state as the wheels thudded beneath me.

A couple of hours went by, when a noise up front alerted me. The sound of coal being shovelled forward. And after a few minutes a head appeared over the top of the coal, and froze! Intently looking towards me, then, "What are you doing there, who's that?" His voice very unsure, surprised. Maybe I was a dead body, a dark lump, or what? I could sense his imagination running wild, peering through a mist of steam and smoke at a large blanket-covered - what?

I poked my dirty head up. "Just travelling", I said, as casually as I could. Though knowing instinctively he wouldn't leave me there.

He was reassured, I was alive. "Come on down, Buddy, you can't stay there", he said in a softer, a relieved, tone.

I climbed down, over the coal, pulling my blanket with me. The fireman had already said a few words to the driver, and as I stepped down on to the footplate behind them he turned from his seat and said, "Sure cold out there, Bud." I nodded in assent.

The fireman had taken his seat on the other side of the furnace, and with a lever had set in motion an automatic coal feeding system. Instead of shovelling coal into the fire, the fuel now came steadily rolling over a moving grid, directly into the furnace. The only manual work involved being, bringing the coal from the rear of the tender towards this contraption. I was fascinated by this moving stream of fuel, as the fireman used the lever to govern and control the rate of flow without leaving his seat. I stood on the confined space of the footplate, holding a metal grip, whilst the heat from the fire roasted me in front, and the icy wind outside revolved around my back.

But the hours and the miles were again slipping by. The two men sitting on their seats, looking through their respective forward portholes, saying nothing, and asking nothing.

Almost another hour went by, when the driver turned to me and said, "We will be stopping shortly for water, a small town. We will be stopped for half an hour. Drop off when we've slowed down, pick us up again a couple of hundred yards the other side of town." "Ok, thanks", I replied.

I rolled my blanket up, attached it as before hanging over my shoulder, and a little later as the train slowed, I jumped off.

There was a country road beside the track, snow covered and empty. Walking towards a small cluster of houses on this late winter afternoon, I soon discovered the general store and bought a loaf of bread, and although the man who served me said nothing, I thought he gave me a strange look. Oh heck! I mused. I stood out as a total stranger in this sleepy little hamlet, he must have wondered where on earth I had come from.

The bread tasted delicious, as eating half of it, I walked through this small village and up the lane, well beyond where the train was standing hissing beside the huge water tank. I stood beside a railway shed waiting for the inevitable double wail of the hooter when the train got under way. I guessed the driver and his mate would not recognise me, or want me near whilst under possibly unfriendly eyes. Their jobs would be at stake if they were caught carrying illegal passengers. It was only too well known that railway workers had some of the few prestigious jobs there were, and although they might have sympathy for anyone in my position, they would never jeopardise their own employment. So whilst there were houses and possibly the odd cop around they would do nothing that might endanger themselves.

Soon came the expected signal. And after the usual juddering and wheel slipping, the motion became smooth as the engine approached. I grabbed a rail and jumped onto the lower step, then up onto the footplate behind the driver. A cursory glance from both men as I appeared. Then the locomotive was picking up speed, and I was roasting in front and freezing behind once more.

It seemed ages. The sun had set, it was dark, just the continuous noise, and the headlights, far more powerful than expected - like speeding into a tunnel of light.

Eventually the train driver turned and said, "You alright? It's about an hour to Ottawa. How far you going?"

"Ottawa will do today, Montreal tomorrow, and England next week", I replied, expecting some response. But no interest was shown. Just a grunt, and back to silence.

Shortly afterwards, I became aware of lights here and there, more habitations, the clatter of points as sidings appeared. We were entering the outskirts of the city, and approaching the marshalling yards. We were slowing down now, gradually the steady rhythm, *tatter de tat, tatter de tat*, of the wheels changed slowly, to a more drawn out tempo.

The driver turned and declared, "Jump as soon as you can, pal, and get away from the railroad, there's plenty of cops round the town." "Thanks for the ride", I said, then stepped down onto the lower step. Soon, when I judged it had slowed sufficiently, I jumped, sprinted down the embankment, off the railroad and on to a side road.

Now I was feeling very confident, as the realisation was beginning to seep through to me that surely the worst was over. Less than two hundred miles to Montreal. Calgary was far far behind me now. I was elated, as I looked back over the last few days, over two thousand miles back, and my hundred dollar roll still intact in my pocket.

I was light of step as I walked towards the centre, the lighted area guiding me. In no time I was in streets with lights and sidewalks and people about. It was then I had a feeling that people were giving me a second look. Every time I passed somebody, I was sure they turned and looked curiously at me.

I had never been in Ottawa before, but I did know all the large towns had small hotels and rooming houses, generally away from the central area. I found a quiet side street where a number of properties advertised '*20 cents a bed, 50 cents a room*', and entered one of them.

A small deformed man sat behind a cramped reception desk.

"Have you got a vacant room?" I enquired.

"No single beds", he said defensively.

"I want a room", I repeated.

"Fifty cents", he said, still on guard.

With which I produced the coins. He took them, got down from his seat, and seemed to disappear, came round in front, then I could see. He was a dwarf, and an aggressive little man at that. He led me along a short dingy corridor, unlocked a door, gave me a key, then walked away.

94

I entered, switched on a light, and had the shock of my life. I was facing a mirror over a washbasin and could see this apparition. I was jet black, like a negro, from my cap downwards, face and neck! No wonder I had been getting some strange looks. No wonder the little man was wary. I hadn't thought that sitting on a coal tender for hours, whilst the steam and smoke swirled over me, would blacken me as surely as though I had been painted. I wondered what the little man might think in the morning, once I had a bath. He had let his room to a negro, and a white man came out the next day.

Coloured faces were a rarity anywhere in Canada. Unofficially, coloureds were not encouraged in at that time, as an African face would draw attention anywhere, though whether I was taken for a negro or a hobo I would never know.

I found the bathroom, had a bath, beat as much of the sooty dust out of my cap and greatcoat as possible, and went to bed. Surprisingly it was very comfortable.

Now I pondered. Tomorrow I would collect my passport and on to Montreal.

***

Again, it seemed a far cry back to Regina, where I had spent my second winter with Karl. We got on well together, doing our bit of cooking, going to the 'movies' about three times a week, when the programmes changed at the three cinemas. I also enjoyed sitting in the library, reading and savouring the comfort. Luckily, being the boss's 'blue eyed boy' there were no problems regarding my small wage, whereas Karl had a fight every week on pay day. He was a very good craftsman, efficient and fast, but he was paid on a semi piecework basis. And on each Friday there would be a slanging match, when the boss disputed Karl's time sheet and figures. They would argue and shout at each other for ten minutes. The boss always won.

Karl liked his job, and knew how scarce jobs were, so gave in. Afterwards there never seemed to be any animosity between them.

The same applied to George the upholsterer, the only difference being that George was only employed irregularly, when the work was there. There were many weeks when he had no work.

George lived in a rooming house with other Germans, and was an ardent Nazi. He ranted on about Hitler, but when he got going, Karl retreated into silence, and didn't hear a thing. The Mounties had been round a couple of times, talking to the boss, and questioning us about Nazi literature.

The boss said, "If he doesn't keep his mouth shut I'll give him the bullet." But he stayed on, he also was a very good worker.

For me it was a very pleasant time. I bought ice skates and learned how to skate. And Karl and I spent many an hour at the weekends, down at the lake. Wascana Lake was a man-made lake in front of the Parliament Buildings, maybe half a mile long and a few hundred yards wide; a boating lake in summer - though I had seen it dried right out during the drought - but in winter a solid sheet of ice; over which one could glide at speed, an exhilarating experience. But on a sunny cold day it became somewhat crowded.

The previous winter I had rather envied Karl his guitar. He played Hawaiian style, across his knees, and with a 'steel'. The strings being plucked with either of three fingers and thumb, with a plectrum on each. So I bought one of the same, and soon became sufficiently proficient for us to play together and amuse ourselves for many evenings with our wailing instruments, often much to the disapproval of Mr. Cinnati.

Mr. Cinnati rented a room, next to ours, from the boss. He was a middle-aged bachelor who, I remember, always wore a dickey tie. What he did for a living we did not know, but he was a professional violinist, belonging to the local orchestra. He would spend many evenings practising, and to us, seemingly the same incomprehensible piece over and over again.

I asked him once if he could play a particular piece of light classical music. I got a haughty, "That is not in my repertoire", in reply. We never did hear him play anything we knew. But we were quite contented with our lighter, popular kind of music.

One evening, late, we had been to the movies, and walking back through the city centre, passed the offices of the local daily paper, " *The Regina Leader Post*". There were always people standing around watching, and inquisitive, as, after dark, above the paper's first floor offices, world news would be flashed on a strip of moving screen. And when news of great importance was anticipated, as was now, at the end of 1931, the crowd would be quite large. The Sino-Japanese crisis had been filling the papers for a long time. After numerous forays into China, tonight we were being told of a full scale offensive, and invasion of China.

Strange, how quiet a crowd will become, when momentous, frightening news is thrust upon them. Events that were, maybe, heralding the beginning of World War Two.

Karl and I were standing, not talking, when the silence was unexpectedly shattered. Someone grabbed my arm with a, "Cor Blimey - if it ain't Bill Warren. Wotcher doing 'ere mate, 'member me?" It was Bob, the cockney of our party of boy immigrants. He was small, he was smartly dressed, and he was loud and irrepressible. During our voyage over, everybody had liked him. "Yes, he's a nice bloke", was the general opinion. But, he *never* stopped talking. His loud, clipped cockney accent just went on and on, needing very little response, just an ear.

But we did have one thing in common. Whereas all the others of our group had had odd jobs, trying one thing or another before emigrating, I had had the beginnings of a trade, working in a piano factory learning the trade of French polishing; and Bob had served three years working as a dental mechanic, and learning that trade in the East End of London.

We bought some beer, and the three of us returned to our comfortable den. We exchanged experiences. His first job on a farm had lasted no longer than mine. The difference being that after just a few weeks, he just packed up and headed straight back to Regina. "Heck! No", farming was not for him, he needed streets and people and town activity. I remember being amazed when he said, "Bill, mate, I couldn't stand all that muck and stink, it's a different smell in the streets back home. Anyhow, got myself a job with a dental mechanic, and that's a year ago. Nice 'ole town this, Regina."

He was my first contact with any of our group of boys, but he had met up with three others, and there were no successful reports. A couple of years later I would run into him again, he never did leave that job. At least Cockney Bob was content with his lot. It was at that time, through him, that I learnt of Harry's death.

Harry, our cabin companion, the Lancashire orphan who was so ill with sea sickness.

He had, apparently, one winter, been working in a lumber camp in Northern Alberta. He had complained of feeling unwell all day. During the night, in the bunkhouse, he had obviously been in great pain. There were no medical services or help within a hundred miles, so nobody could do anything. In the morning he was found dead in his bunk.

Later the authorities had his body brought to Regina for burial. He had died of acute appendicitis. Bob had attended the funeral, and said "they", the powers that be, had failed to locate any relatives.

A sad short life. "Our Harry", an unknown, interred in alien soil.

That winter was a severe one, with the temperatures dropping constantly below zero Fahrenheit. Economic activity was nil, and the war in China filled the newspapers. Not that we could avoid political talk, with George forever spreading his Nazi propaganda. Karl did have his antidote. He used to go to meetings of the German speaking group. The outcome of which would often be, maybe once a week, he would say, "Say, Bill, going to the movies tonight?" If I said I probably was, he would say, "Don't rush back, I've got Irma coming to see me tonight." It was always a different name, and I seldom saw them, these girls, as I stayed till the cinema closed. Karl was a few years older than me, and he was always offering to introduce me to German girls. But his casualness with women was "off putting" to me, and I never took his offers up.

The winter passed, but unlike Karl I had become restless. Whilst he remained content at the bench, I needed to move on.

One day at the end of March I said, "Mr. Surtees, I've got a job on a farm, I'll be leaving next week." "Ok, Bill", he accepted, "keep in touch."

Again I went by train to a little town called Lipton, where I had hired out for the season to Sam Wheale. Only ten dollars a month this year, because everywhere wages and prices were falling, as the depression bit deeper all the time.

Most of the snow had gone, and Sam met me with a wagon on wheels, to drive north to his farm, fifteen miles away. Sam was completely different to any farmers of my previous experience. He looked big, all bundled up, but somewhat ungainly. No nonsense about call me Sam, or anything else. Just a, "Hello, you Bill, my team's outside." And we were off. He was English and had emigrated to Canada during the early part of the century; he had worked for many years in Ontario, then just after the First World War had homesteaded in Saskatchewan. We were now on the way to that same homestead, and Sam put me in the picture regarding his farm, whilst chewing a plug of tobacco, and spitting between times.

I had a shock when we approached his farm. So different to any of my previous homes. A small log shack consisting of two smallish rooms. Mrs. Wheale and her three young children came out to see what the new 'hired man' looked like, and we all crowded inside rather awkwardly. It was all quite easy and informal. Although Sam's wife was somewhat dishevelled and almost shy I liked her immediately; the three kids stood around, quiet and shyly, Mary about eleven, Ben eight and Helen five. The atmosphere was homely, but far from affluent. The main room was the living room, with a door leading off to the bedroom where the entire family slept. A ladder led up to the attic, where I was to sleep.

'Aw heck! Everybody seems friendly, maybe this will be a good job.'

Sam showed me around and explained his procedure, and what I had to do. He did not call me at five in the morning, instead his wife called up to the attic at six o'clock, and I rose and did all the usual farm chores of milking, feeding, grooming horses and so on. I returned to breakfast about seven thirty, by which time Sam had stirred, and would come into the living room, yawning and stretching. No! Sam was not a typical Canadian farmer. He plodded, he liked to get going slowly; though once land work started, he might be the last farmer around to get going in the morning, late evening would find him still working when all the others had long since had their suppers and were thinking of bed.

Sam's holding of a half section of land, 320 acres, was just beyond the northern edge of the true prairies. North now for two hundred miles or more was rolling parkland type of country, with thick standings of poplars and willows. Many 'sloughs', that is, small lakes or ponds, which generally dried out by June or July, and provided a luscious crop of hay. All the fuel came from the clumps of poplar scattered around the farm. This area was very picturesque and although the road allowances were religiously adhered to, north, south, and east, west, the fields, of necessity took on irregular shapes. So different to the vastness of the prairie just a few miles away. Sam had only been partly affected by the drought of the previous year. A poor crop, but worth harvesting. Now was another year, though 'drought' was still the major talking point.

The horses had been rounded up and brought inside the week before I arrived. As usual at this time of year, they were fat and woolly from foraging all winter, and very frisky. One had to be very careful with the handling of them, until once again they were broken in to harness and work. In Sam's small log barn they had an unnerving tendency to kick out backwards just as one was passing, and during the first few days I had to move very sharply many a time.

Land work quickly commenced, as with the short spring, the remains of the snow melted, the temperature rose fast, and I settled into a routine. Day in, day out, I drove an outfit of six horses, disking ahead of Sam's seed drill, which in turn was pulled by six horses. At this time of year everything was fresh and verdant; I enjoyed the outdoor life and was as thrilled as anybody, when out of the south the Canadian geese arrived. Flying high and plaintively honking as they flew in their vee formation, powering relentlessly northwards in their instinctive need to propagate the species. Harbingers of spring and new life, they would not stop until they reached their nesting grounds on the edge of the Arctic. Returning late in the year to wintering areas in the southern states with their new broods.

Time never seemed to matter to Sam except for in the mornings, and late in the day, I felt niggly at having no set time to work to. So after a week of uncertainty I said, "Sam, what time am I supposed to work to?" He was quite hurt and surprised, I don't think he had ever thought about it. "Oh! Six o'clock, alright." I was relieved, and though I had no watch, the sun was always up there, and I could judge the time near enough and leave the field with a clear conscience, whilst Old Sam plodded steadily on.

"Old Sam" - I don't suppose he was more than fifty - with his craggy face, and just a few odd teeth which made him look old, also all his movements were stiff. When I had first arrived, I wondered what the two ropes suspended over an old sofa beside the wall, were for. I soon got used to him; in the late evening, he would stretch out on this particular sofa, then put on the earphones of his wireless set, lay back and enjoy whatever was being broadcast. His face often creasing up as he chuckled - at we knew not what. Funny, when he smiled the years dropped away, or appeared to and he was no longer leathery "Old Sam".

It was when he went to rise, that the ropes came into play. He grasped them and struggled to pull himself up, invariably saying, "Old joints are a bit rheumatic tonight". He did have a dry sense of humour, because often he would say as he pulled himself up, "Jesus! I can't ride tonight", or some other such crack, whilst he was obviously in considerable pain.

During the first few weeks, the evenings being cold, I was in the habit of sitting in my attic room, strumming my guitar, practising.

One day Sam said, "You can practise down here if you like." I felt rather self-conscious, but one cold evening thought, why not? The large wood burning range that was always well stacked up was a great attraction also. The living room, although sparsely furnished was very comfy with a number of comfortable chairs. When I came down, Sam as usual, "was listening in", he couldn't hear anything else when his earphones were on. So I sat and strummed a few bars.

There was one particular piece of music which I had practised at, and with that one piece I was confidently proficient. So I settled down and played my "party piece", the Spanish Fandango. The kids went quiet and suddenly Old Sam removed his headphones, and when I had finished asked, "What was that called?" I told him. He said, "I liked that, play it again." So for the first time I had an audience, and felt really flattered. He had removed his earphones, and thereafter whenever I brought my guitar down he lay on his back listening to me, and mostly I was just practising.

A job I was offered and quickly took up, was collecting the mail. Two miles away was the Leslies' farm. Mr. and Mrs. Leslie had no children. They were Scottish immigrants, with accents so strong they were hard to understand, not that Mr. Leslie ever said anything, his wife said it all, her chatter was endless. They had a half section farm, but also their farm was a country post office. "The Headlands P.O.". Mr. Leslie would go into town, Lipton, deliver mail, and collect all the mail for the surrounding area. This was on a Friday, every week, so their farm became a gathering point on Friday nights.

That particular evening of the week I really looked forward to. After supper I would saddle Lucy, a lovely pitch black riding horse, and go and collect any mail there might be. I knew there would be my regular letter from home. And also, it was very agreeable, meeting the many farmers' sons and hired men who rode over for the same purpose. I quickly got to know many of them.

One particular farmer's son, a Ukrainian named Ivan - *I am not Russian* - and I, seemed to have a special rapport; we nattered away, and one day discovered we had a mutual pleasure in the game of chess.

Mrs. Leslie, who was always in on every conversation said, "Bring your chess set, and play here." Which we did.

102

Mrs. Leslie set us up on her kitchen table, fussing around and plying us with coffee; she had no idea of the game. We were evenly matched, so many a game went on until late, to the sound of her clicking knitting needles and an occasional, "Is that the same game? Tut, tut." Whilst Old Mr. Leslie sat nodding and dreaming by the wood stove, never saying a word, but silently topping our coffee cups whenever he came out of his dreams, or putting another log on the fire.

I soon came to realise they were the "salt of the earth", because of his regularity and reliability in going to town. Everybody said, "Ask Old Leslie, he will get it, or he will do it,"; he never demurred, whenever something was required.

Much later in the year, I was still comfortably settled with Sam and his family. It was a Friday night in December, and I was preparing to collect the mail. It was cold and snowing. Sam said, "You shouldn't go out tonight, there's a blizzard on the way, said so on the wireless."

Blizzards are dangerous, he was right of course.

But I wanted my game, "I'll be alright", I said. He didn't attempt to dissuade me.

Shortly afterwards, dressing well against the weather, I went and saddled Lucy, and trotted off on my two mile trip. There was quite a wind, making it feel very cold, and although the temperature was only ten degrees below freezing, the wind factor made it appear much colder and thus more dangerous.

The track was good for a mile, but then one had to ride across a mile of virgin prairie, undeveloped land, straight towards a light in the distance. That light was in a window of the Leslie farm. No problem! I arrived, put Lucy in the barn, and enjoyed two hours of playing chess.

In the meantime the wind had built up to blizzard force. Old Mr. Leslie advised, "Better bunk down on the floor till daylight." Ivan had already decided to stay, but he lived over five miles away.

"Thanks, no, I'll get going", I said. "S'long, folks", as I donned my

103

outside clothes, and struggled out to the barn. Resaddled Lucy, and out into the snow. I found the yard gate with great difficulty, secured it behind us and remounted Lucy.

Old Mr. Leslie had just shrugged and conveyed a "suit yourself" attitude when I said I was going, and now I understood why. I only had to ride a mile straight ahead to the track. Only! Within a few minutes I was hopelessly disorientated, the whirling snow buffeting from every angle quickly confused one's sense of direction, and the cold soon attacked one's extremities. It seemed that I was riding in circles and that hours and hours had gone by; the cold was permeating my whole body. I was really worried, but Lucy just put her head down and plodded on.

In the winter, the prairie newspapers were continually printing stories of people being caught in blizzards and quickly freezing to death. During my first winter in Regina, I well remember the story of how a car had been caught in snow drifts just outside the city. The four occupants had decided to sit it out, and had left the engine running to keep the heater going. The next morning they were all found dead, *not* from cold, but from carbon monoxide poisoning.

I only had to worry about how the icy cold was penetrating my bones. The short journey should have taken half an hour. It seemed I was going through a white milling eternity for ever.

When, suddenly, Lucy stopped, and there was our yard gates. I could now discern, through the milky whiteness, a lantern swinging. In the house porch Sam was standing. "You alright, Bill", he said nonchalantly, "thought it was getting late, go in, I'll see to Lucy."

Mrs.Wheale - I never knew her first name - fussed around me, coffee instantly in my hands. And I hugged the fire to get the ice out of my system. But what a relief! Phones had been ringing, I had taken an hour and a half instead of half an hour. Opinions had no doubt been voiced over the air about my obstinate stupidity, but for sure, I had also created a talking point for days to come.

Every farm, however humble, had a phone. There might be no running water, electricity or sewage, but a phone - yes. This was how they all kept in touch. There were a large number of farms to each local line, and when the phone rang, everybody would wait to hear the appropriate number of rings. If it was the correct number, your own number, you lifted the receiver and had your conversation. If not, one would say "so and so is getting a call." Often during a conversation one would hear a *click* and know that someone was listening in, many a foul word was used at these unknown eavesdroppers. To make a call, one had to pick up the receiver, then turn a handle, each complete turn being one ring. All calls, other than those on one's local line, had to go through an operator.

The phone rang many times late that evening, asking about my where-abouts. It would appear there had been a lot of "listening in" earlier.

Praise was heaped upon Lucy. I had heard about horses heading straight for home. Making a beeline, people said. I doubt the beeline, but she had proved her ability to find her way home, when I was hopelessly lost. In fact Lucy was a very reliable, docile mare, plus being a very good worker. She would allow one to take a bridle out to her when she was in the pasture, place it on her without objection, and jump on her bare back. Not many horses would allow that.

But all animals are different, most have some distinguishing idiosyncrasy, and Lucy had an unusual one.

A few miles away, a farmer, Pete Herman, was the owner of a shire stallion. A beautiful, black, massive animal. Arrogant and proud. During spring, and on into late summer, every few weeks he would make his rounds. If a farmer had a mare in season, or coming into season, he would call and service her. These calls would be organised over the phone, as a mare would normally remain in condition for a few days.

Sam had half a dozen mares, two of which he had been trying to breed for a few years, without success.

"Lady" was a jet black highly spirited horse, nervous, a hard worker;

she would pour with sweat and be quite hard to control. "Nora" was the opposite, black, but quiet and placid, a plodding worker.

There came a day in spring when Lady was ready, and Nora also coming into season, and coinciding with the stallion's tour of duty.

Mr. Herman, the proud owner of this great prancing beast who was called "Roger", drove a wagon with a team of horses, and had Roger, tied with a lead at the back. By the time they were within half a mile of the farm, all the horses were responding in various ways to the almost continuous neighing of his lord and master as he drew near. Those tied up in the barn were teetering and snorting, everyone on the pitch of alertness. But most of the geldings out in the pasture were nervous and frightened - many horses after being castrated change to an enormous degree and become quite fearful when a stallion is around.

Lady had been tied to a post in the yard on a fairly long lead. After the usual chat and preliminaries were over, Roger was led towards the mare, also on a long lead. Lady resisted, kept prancing and being temperamental, laying her ears back, bucking and jumping about.

One of Sam's children, young Len, suddenly appeared from the house, on some errand. Sam immediately shouted at him to go back in, and that none of the kids were to come out till he said so. He seemed embarrassed; they all grew up with animals and learnt as they grew, but horses were different. Strange things took place when the "Rogers" of the world were around; not for childish eyes, there was a little more to the "act", as Lady was proving, with her coquettish behaviour.

However after a while, Pete, who was becoming impatient and worried by the mare's constant bucking and rampaging said, "If she kicks once again, we will stop trying, I'm not having Roger injured." She did eventually, suddenly, allow Roger to ride, and became instantly quiet. Then Nora was serviced without bother.

In the meantime, Lucy, who was tied up in the barn with other horses, had been neighing and fretting, rolling her eyes, curling her lips and generally making a nuisance of herself, teetering irritably.

Pete said, "The old girl's at it again."

We were sitting smoking and chatting for half an hour. Sam said doubtfully, "Whilst you're here, might as well try again." He had been trying to breed Lucy for years. She appeared to come into season at the sound of a stallion.

She was led out, no need to tie her; Roger performed his act professionally and without hesitation. Lucy's face took a foolish look as she rolled her eyes, and Sam said disdainfully, "Randy bitch!" Once again Lucy did not produce, but nearly a year later Lady gave birth to a beautiful black foal, as did Nora.

Sam was always talking of the house he was going to build, and the year prior to my appearing on the scene, he had cleared a wooded site, about fifty feet from his present log cabin, and dug his basement. This was quite a feat in itself: a hole, maybe twenty feet by fifteen, and about seven feet deep. All houses, large or small had basements. They probably originated with the need to store food away from the severe frosts. So a hole in the ground with a house above was ideal. Sam's present basement was literally a basic store room. Whereas many people lined them, turning them into useful extra rooms.

Sam's intention was to erect a log house over this large excavation. He had, the previous winter, journeyed fifty or more miles north to where the true forest began, where he could fell trees with the girth necessary for building logs, then manhandle them into his wagon, which at that time of year was on sleighs. He could only transport six trees at a time. Trunks twenty feet or more long, with diameters of eighteen inches were a heavy load. But a wagon on sleds could take a much greater load than one on wheels.

However, the weather had to be right, many other things had to be arranged, so his trips of three or four days were few and far between. And when would he finally get round to building was questioned with cynicism by many of the local farmers.

Later in the year he decided to make one of these trips. The snow was deep, the weather settled, when one evening Sam queried, "You can look after things for a few days, Bill?" "Of course", I said. I was only too pleased to be left in charge. Land work was finished till the spring, the majority of the horses had been turned out for the winter; they would once again grow fat and semi-wild, their freedom could last until April came round again. Two teams of horses were kept in, to do the chores and winter work. Sam would be taking Charlie and Roy, a pair of beautiful sorrel gelding shires, imposing in their strength, and Sam's pride and joy. I would be left with Lucy and Nora.

Sam left in the early hours next day. I did my usual milking, feeding and cleaning, and after breakfast, when I came out to do a spell at the wood pile splitting logs, I glanced at the thermometer and noticed it was twenty degrees below zero F; but the sun was shining, it was very still, and splitting logs was an invigorating occupation. Most of the days at this time of year were spent out in the bluffs, felling trees and hauling them back to the farmhouse. Where every few weeks a farmer owning a circular saw and tractor would come round and spend a day reducing trees to logs. Filling in time was always spent at the woodpile splitting endless piles of logs, for the insatiable wood stove.

The next morning the temperature remained the same. It was still and bright as I entered the barn to start milking. Inside the building the atmosphere was very warm, humid and fuggy. There were six cows in the stalls down one side, only three of which were in milk. Lucy and Nora were in the stalls on the opposite side. Nora was still lying down, which wasn't unusual, so I proceeded to milk the cows. It wasn't until I had milked the first cow, that something made me feel there was something wrong. I put the bucket down and went over to Nora, and tapping her with my boot said, "Come on, old girl, time to get up." A slight response, her head half lifted from where it was nuzzled down on her shoulder, but no more. I knew then something was definitely wrong. I tried again, pushing her head, shouting at her, anything to get some reaction, but to no avail.

She was not rising, and common sense told me something serious was the matter. I finished the milking, wondering what to do. I was out of my depth, I hadn't a clue.

I returned to the house. Mrs. Wheale was cooking breakfast, the kids milling around. She always appeared flustered at this time of day, a somewhat timid type of woman. I really had very little contact with her, and although she was forever working, there was a shyness whenever she needed to speak to me.

Now, when I voiced my fears, and explained to her that Nora could not get up and so something must be seriously wrong, she responded straight away. "We will have to get Bud, he'll know what to do, it's probably colic." This was a term bandied about by all the farmers. One could just have easily said the animal is sick or ill. However, there were no vets around for hundreds of miles, so anybody who had any knowledge of animal husbandry, or professed to have, would be called upon.

Bud was one of those garrulous little men, who made himself known and liked by everyone. He lived in a small shack with his wife and two kids. His cabin was on somebody else's land. He owned nothing except for a horse and buggy, which gave him mobility. And he worked on any farm that needed him.

Sam's wife quickly phoned the farmer, on whose land Bud lived; he in turn said he would contact Bud straight away. Within an hour, this small weather beaten man, with his equally small but wiry horse, came trotting into the yard, the buggy now on sleds, the wheels having been removed for winter.

I liked Bud, Sam often had jobs for him to do, so he was no stranger. Everybody liked Bud; he was probably forty, but facially looked a lot older. He was capable, worked hard. But if there was anybody around he never stopped talking. I think that was one of his great assets. Amongst a mainly dour and taciturn bunch of farmers, he stood out.

"It's Nora, is it?", he said, "let's have a look." Without more ado we entered the barn. He also seemed to know every horse's name for miles around, he was always involved, he didn't just work for someone. He became included in everything going on, and of course he had an opinion about every imaginable thing.

He talked to the horse, "Nora, you can't lay there, work to do", as he wandered around sizing up the situation. "I don't know what's the matter with you, but I know you've got to get to your feet, old girl. All animals die when they lie down and give up."

He was talking his thoughts, but Nora made no response.

He made a decision. "Bill, I know where I can borrow a cradle, block and tackle; I'll be back within an hour, keep talking to the mare, keep her awake." He jumped into his buggy and was gone. I told Mrs. Wheale; she said, "Stay with Nora, I'll help when he gets back."

An hour later he was back. Loaded down with this contraption, the working of which he proceeded to explain to me. A large section of reinforced canvas, with long straps affixed to four corners. He had already noted a large log beam above Nora's stall. This would take the block and tackle, which in turn would be fixed to the straps, and then with the ratchet action of the block and tackle the horse would be slowly helped to her feet. Easy to fix the tackle ready for the operation. The problem was getting the cradle under the mare in the first place.

Fortunately Mrs. Wheale suddenly appeared with, "Can I help?", and during the next few minutes proved her ability as a farmer's wife.

Nora was slumped right down on her belly, head tucked in, wanting only to be alone.

"Now", said Bud, "this is the tricky bit, we have to be cruel to be kind. Bill, and you, Ada - that sounded rather strange - be ready to push the cradle under her, as soon as there's space. Right!" Suddenly he started shouting at her, *gid up, gid up, gid up*, and pulling and pushing at her head at the same time, never stopping, shouting right into her ear, and amazingly she was struggling to get to her feet. Down she went, then nearly up, then down again. Then another effort, eyes dilating as she made the final endeavour, and we managed at last to get the cradle under her.

Bud said, "Now, no stopping halfway, you can take the strain on the pulley, Bill. Ada, keep lightly kicking her backside. And Bill, don't stop pulling till she's on her feet. Right!" Then once again he was pulling her head, shouting and exciting her. She struggled, bringing her legs forward; the effort was coming as she heaved herself upward, whilst I was frantically tugging at the rope governing the hoist. And then it all came together, one final surge, she was up, and I had the cradle taut beneath her.

She was standing! Legs quivering and body trembling, but now she would not be allowed to give in or lay down until she was well, *or?* When she had calmed a little, Bud tried her with some tepid water; she drank a little, her head was still drooping, and Bud pronounced, "If it's colic, I know what to do, if it's anything else…", he just shrugged.

Later he mixed his own concoction of mash. Nora was not interested, but late in the day she did eat some, and the following day. Although she was still a very sick horse there was an obvious improvement. The third day when Bud turned up in the morning he said, "I think she's Ok now, but keep her in the cradle till tomorrow, when Sam will be back. I don't want her to go down again." Sam was back the next evening, pleased with his load of logs, and far more interested in the house he was going to build, than about Nora. And talking about going north again in a few weeks' time.

I think the pioneer was still in there, struggling to get out. Like most of the settlers in the area, lumbering, felling trees, clearing land, driving through snow, were all the very essence of the wilderness that had to be tamed when they first arrived. So Sam, like many others had acquired the taste once again. And when his wife went into great detail about Nora's sickness and the time and effort we had spent saving her, Sam still had a faraway look in his eyes. "Sure", he said, "if anybody could save her Bud could, he's a great guy." But he soon turned the conversation round to the North, where the trees are big. Really big!

Nora recovered.

111

It was a few days after this event; the temperature remained well below zero, and I was out felling trees, maybe half a mile from the farm. When unexpectedly I noticed a movement amongst the scrub and tightly packed trees. During the winter animal life was almost nonexistent, and except for the occasional snowbird or chickadee there was never any movement. So I was intrigued to see a black and white animal, as big as a large dog, walking casually and seemingly aimlessly, through the trees. I started walking towards it, out of sheer curiosity, but as I approached, it scampered off, across snowdrifts; whilst I floundered in them, in an effort to get close, it was soon gone.

Later in the day when I returned to the house and was telling my tale Sam said, "Sure lucky you didn't get near it, that was a skunk, and you would have been stinking to high heaven by now; keep clear of those creatures."

But it was a handsome beast.

Sam had a fair crop that year, and for once I had a few dollars, and could treat myself to some typically Canadian gaudy check shirts, ordered through the mail order catalogue - the prairie bible - that supplied everything imaginable; it was the one book that was opened and read and reread on every farm.

Further south, on the plains, the drought had persisted. Brown and barren land, derelict and boarded farms had begun to appear.

After the harvest, Sam's loads of wheat only fetched rock bottom prices, as the depression persisted without sign of change, and life on the farms was at subsistence level only. I never saw Sam buy anything that wasn't absolutely necessary, and during the harvest, when we worked from dawn to dusk, it was surprising how capable the two children were. Len and Mary, even at that early age were adept at milking, and as far as I know, made no bones about getting up in the morning and doing all their chores before walking a mile to school. Sam also got up early at harvest time.

Harvest had a sense of fulfilment. Whether good or bad, it was the end of the farming year. And although it seemed pointless 'producing' at such uneconomically low prices, it was more than money, it was a way of life, and Sam seemed to accept it philosophically, as he chewed away at his tobacco. He didn't need a scapegoat as Gustav the Swede had.

There was a strong community spirit in the area. Particularly at harvest time, when everyone was working flat out. Once the grain was cut and stooked, one of the bigger farmers in the district who owned a threshing machine, would make the rounds of all the farmers within reasonable distance, threshing their crops. This, for a few days, entailed work for at least half a dozen men, working ceaselessly throughout the day. Generally, four men - each with a team of horses and a hay rack - would load the sheaves, and when they had a full load, would drive it to the thresher, sited in the middle of the field, and pitch them onto the moving belt into the machine. The machine must be continuously fed, otherwise it was losing time and money. So as soon as one was unloaded, off he would trot for another load; the four men working in rotation kept this up all day.. And it was a matter of pride that one *did* keep up.

The owner of the machine was controlling and supervising the operation. Two other men had a team and wagon each. The grain was pouring steadily from a large pipe into the wagon. The minute a wagon was full the driver would trot to the farm yard and shovel it into a granary. By the time he returned the other man would be away doing the same. And so it kept up all day. Food and drink would be brought out from the farmhouse, and come evening the sun never set fast enough.

This was a necessary and very sensible community system, and worked very well. I would be working on many different farms at this time - in return for all the men's days spent on our farm.

During harvest time, huge piles of straw would blossom around the farms. The thresher blew the straw out of a long pipe at the side. So wherever it had been at work, straw piles the size of houses were left standing, and in the fall when the land work ceased, they would be burnt. A little would be saved for winter animal bedding, but the rest was commercially useless. For a time it would again cause tongues to wag at such waste, but nobody knew of an alternative use, so the burning persisted.

After harvest there was a period of quietness, as the days shortened and 'fall' was upon us. Many days Sam would be off for the day, to town with a wagon of wheat, and I would be disking, or in some places ploughing with my five or six horses outfit. Sam still believed in the plough, but it was only a matter of time. By September the nights were cold, and in October the frosts were heavier each night, till by November, the temperature would drop consistently to the depth of winter by February.

I remember that particular February, when each morning the outside thermometer read thirty below zero Fahrenheit, without changing for three weeks, the heatless sun shining all day; and when Mrs. Wheale called me each morning and I crawled out of bed, the horse hide covering my bed would be coated in thick white frost.

I had stayed with Sam. After the harvest he had said, "I can't pay you after September, but if you like to stay for your board, we can take up the government scheme for the winter."

I now had a girlfriend. The local schoolteacher who boarded with the Barton family, whose farmhouse could be seen a mile away. So I wanted to stay around.

The government scheme, to keep hired help on the farms, was now well known - paying five dollars per month to hired man and farmer - and used by many farmers, especially in winter, when they would not normally employ labour, but now did. So this would be my first winter on a farm.

In complete contrast to Sam, was Cliff Barton. Cliff lived on the next section. His house, another log house, was perched on top of a small hill, and after dark we could see the light in his windows a mile away. His house had a main living room, a lean-to kitchen, and a small lean-to bedroom. A flight of stairs from the living room led to the first floor, where there were another two small bedrooms. All quite snug, with a large circular wood burning stove in the middle of the main room.

Why Cliff had built his house on top of an exposed hill, nobody knew. Most of the log houses around were built on the level, generally alongside a large bluff, for protection in winter. It was surmised, by some of the locals, that maybe Cliff had arrived in June, and had been plagued by mosquitoes or flies, both of which were a serious pest in early summer, and generally reckoned to be worse on the low ground than the high.

Or maybe he had visions of an Englishman's castle, perched on top of a hill. Because Cliff was the very epitome of the picture usually imagined of an English gentleman. He was slim, blond and blue eyed, well dressed at all times, and spoke with a public school accent. He also was an immigrant to the 'west' following the First World War, had married an attractive Canadian girl in the twenties, and now had two young children. Dawn the eldest, and Jeffrey.

Cliff came from Yorkshire, was well read, a good conversationalist, but whether he actually was educated at a public school I never knew, even though he always wore a collar and tie, even milking the cows. There was a warmth about him and his family that was irresistible. He had a dry sense of humour, and a very wide vocabulary, which sometimes made his wife squirm uncomfortably in her chair, straight-faced, as he would do recitations, full of long words and of a risqué character, with double meanings that made everybody else curl up, at the many house parties and school concerts that were held during the winter months.

Also the Bartons had a piano. And that itself set them apart from the average farmer. Mrs. Barton played well, and often. She was, at most times, rather a reticent and prim woman, but nevertheless tough and matter of fact: when in the normal course of events a pig or other animal had to be slaughtered, she would play her part. She was purposeful, and would do battle with a blizzard if it was necessary to pick the children up from school in a horse sleigh. And to add just a little more to their status, was the fact that the young school teacher, Glenda Wood - who presided over about twenty children of varying ages in an isolated one room schoolhouse - boarded with them.

Whilst at Sam's, and through collecting the mail each week, I got to know many local people, and was often invited out on a Sunday to one of the many scattered farms around.

I was soon invited to the Bartons, and so met Glenda. Even during the summer there were occasional school dances, and I started escorting Glenda to any such event. I would saddle and ride Lucy, meet Glenda at the Barton farm, she would be riding one of Cliff's horses, and we would go the few minutes to the school.

These dances were a big occasion; in summer it was mostly young folk who attended. But in winter when there were far more of them, they became a family affair, with saddled horses, buggies and sleighs, all lined up at the long hitching rail in a big open shed in the school yard. Families and couples would come from miles around, intent on having a good time, and with no intention of going home till four or five o'clock the next morning.

The school house consisted of one large room. It would have been cleared, all desks piled at one end, chairs all round the walls. Oil lamps would be hanging from rafters at each end, and the fiddlers already tuning up.

Sometimes an accordionist, or a banjo player would join them, but two or three fiddlers generally supplied the music and the beat.

At a large wood burning stove at one end of the room, two or three farmers' wives would already be stoking the fire and boiling water, preparatory to making the strong coffee that would be available all night. There would be a break at midnight when everyone produced their own pies and refreshments, and drank endless cups of coffee. But except for an occasional slow waltz, it was an activity evening. The pace was fast right from the beginning. When the request came:

"Take your partners for the first square," the fiddlers struck up, into a beat, as the 'caller' started chanting his directions in a sing song voice.

"Honour your partners, corners address,
Join your hands, go way to the west."

Then one stanza after another. Simple hypnotic directions. We would all sweat and dance the night away.

The square dances, by far the most popular, would every once in a while give way to a foxtrot, waltz or quickstep. Then the lads would have a chance to squeeze up to their partners, the music would slow down, the 'caller' had a rest, then after a slow waltz the 'caller' would once again order us to:

"Take your partners for the next square."

And again to his directions we would be circling and turning, endlessly threading up and down to the simple repetitious music, until, maybe by four o'clock in the morning we would dance the last waltz. Then, exhilarated, we would go our separate ways, and drive or ride home. Often just in time to change one's clothes and start milking or doing the other regular chores.

These dances were a fairly regular Friday night event, though they were interspersed by an occasional amateur concert, and 'auction' or 'pie dances'. These pie dances were very popular with the young folk. The dances started normally. But after maybe an hour, everybody being well warmed up, the caller would stop the music, and direct all the farmers' daughters and hired girls to one end of the room, sitting decorously with their pies on their laps, often quite self-conscious and somewhat embarrassed. All the young bloods would be ranged at the other end of the hall. This was then their opportunity to partner a girl of their choice.

The caller would then commence the auction.

"Now what am I bid for this delicious blueberry pie", or lemon pie, or coconut, "made by pretty Rosie", or whatever was the girl's name. Somebody would offer a "quarter", then the bidding would rise by a few cents a time. Obviously the pie was unimportant, it was the seemingly demure damsel on whose lap it rested who mattered. The contest was therefore rather one sided, as two or three particularly attractive girls received the maximum attention.

I got carried away myself at one such dance; there was an especially delectable lass whose 'pie' I coveted and bid for. After quite a lengthy auction I had spent a dollar, and had the privilege of being presented with the pie by this same young lady. We found chairs, she cut a portion of pie and we proceeded to eat. To my small talk she did not respond and just smiled shyly. Anyhow the music had started up for a foxtrot; I intimated, shall we dance. We took to the floor; she danced well but without words, something was sadly lacking. It wasn't until we danced close by one of my friends, amongst all the music and chatting that he quietly said, "She doesn't speak English, she's Ukrainian."

When the music ended, I was only too pleased to escort her back to her group of parents and other brothers and sisters. The smile was a permanent feature of her face, very pretty, but I felt it had been a some-what wasted effort. The pie was nice, but heck! I'd certainly got nowhere with the girl. I didn't even know her name.

The little money raised by these auctions went to a small fund, held by one of the farmers, who was also a school governor. It helped cover the cost of lighting and heating, and others small outgoings. The school itself was a focus point, and used for many events apart from schooling. The area was thinly populated, and Glenda, the school teacher - who was only twenty herself - had to teach twenty to twenty-five children, whose ages ranged from five to fifteen years. They travelled up to five miles each day, and many had little or no English.

She had many problems.

It was towards the end of the year with Sam. I had driven with Glenda to a dance in a one-horse, comfortable little buggy on sleds. We had danced all night, and in the early hours of the morning had just left the school yard to return home, when from a nearby copse came such an unearthly scream, my hair stood on end, and Glenda clung to me in fright. "What the heck was that?" I queried. After a few minutes Glenda relaxed and replied, "It took me by surprise, I should have known better, it was a lynx." Of all the animals I had heard of, that was new to me. Apparently they were around, but very rare and seldom seen.

The locals had a tendency to throw people together.

It was midwinter of the following year, February, when Cliff Barton said to me, "You could come and work for me for a couple of

118

months. Ask Sam, I don't think he will mind. The government grant can be transferred."

Sam was easy, "Sure, Bill, you can come back in the spring if you wish."

I spent the remainder of a memorable winter with them. Cliff did not employ any labour in the normal course of events. He only owned a quarter section, one hundred and sixty acres, and as a family they were really quite poor, but somehow it did not show. Mrs. Barton was very house proud, the kids always neatly dressed, and of course, Cliff was immaculate at all times, and Glenda who boarded with them was a financial asset, and the reason that I accepted Cliff's offer so cheerfully.

There was a sense of home from home in the Barton household. Most Fridays - and I don't know why it was always Fridays - come evening time the horses would be hitched to the sleigh, and the family, plus Glenda and myself, would be off to a dance, or now in late winter, to one of the many house parties.

These house parties were held at the larger farms in the neighbourhood. A different farm each time. The Barton never held one themselves, but were always invited. Mrs. Barton, for her ability on the piano, and Cliff for his sparkling personality. All night long we young ones would dance to the beat of fiddle or piano, and in another room all the older folk would be playing cards. Auction bridge being the popular and favourite card game at the time.

All guests would bring pies and cookies, with the host supplying the inevitable coffee. The jollifications would end at about four or five o'clock, still long before daylight at this time of year, and like the dances, everybody would return to their farms in time for milking. Then after breakfast, on with the normal chores of a winter's day.

When I went inside for midday dinner after one of these parties, I noticed, a little resentfully, that Cliff wasn't around. But of course, I realised magnanimously, he was forty. He was old, and had to have a few hours' sleep! Whereas I was a conceited youth, cockily proud of being able to go without a night's sleep.

During the short winter's afternoon, in sub-zero temperatures I would be kept occupied. Feeding all the animals that had to be kept inside at this time of year. Clearing out the endless accumulations of manure. Splitting logs for the voracious wood stove, milking, and all the other odds and ends that make up a winter day's work.

Then, all finished, animals bedded down for the night, getting dark!

In for supper.

But this particular evening, no radio, no piano. BED! To sleep like a log immediately.

Then Cliff calling out. "Bill, it's six o'clock." It was Sunday morning, still pitch dark and freezing hard, as I made my way out to the barn to start milking. As elsewhere, only essential chores were done on Sundays, the Bartons being regular church-goers. So after breakfast we all changed into our best clothes, hitched the team to the sleigh and off to church.

The majority of the homesteaders in this district were English, with a minority made up of Germans, Ukrainians, Poles and a few Scots. They seemed to form small colonies, with a tendency to cling together. But whether they were religious or not, they all seemed to gather on a Sunday, at this small wooden protestant church, built comparatively recently - in the twenties - and like the schoolhouse a focus point for the mixed surrounding farming community.

After the hymns and service, in late morning, the farmers, their families and hired help, would gather in small groups and talk 'pigs and cows'. The young blades would ogle the girls, the girls would be all 'coy'. And Mrs. Barton would cast black looks in Cliff's direction, who would be shining with charisma, sparkling, in a group of females. Whilst I would think he was a real swell guy, but far too old at forty to be any real competition.

Sunday evenings was always a sing song. Mrs. Barton was well up with all the latest hits. She enjoyed playing the piano, and we all enjoyed singing, "Home on the range", or, "When it's springtime in the Rockies". They also had a radio set with a loud speaker, which was really 'something' at that time, and Mrs. Barton had a knack of quickly picking out a new tune, so we would learn all the 'latest hits'. Not that there was any hurry, a popular new song would last for months and months, and the radio would play a really appealing air, incessantly.

I thoroughly enjoyed the few months I stayed with the Bartons. But come the spring, I returned and worked for Sam again.

In the early part of summer, Glenda and I conspired together, to have a weekend in Regina. Although we were going steady, it would certainly not have been approved of by the adult community, especially for a schoolteacher; she would be expected to uphold the somewhat puritanical atmosphere which prevailed amongst 'country folk'.

A "World Grain Exhibition" was to be held in Regina in June, and was big news throughout Saskatchewan and Canada. With this as a lever, I approached Sam for a few days holiday, - holidays were unheard of - he knew that everyone around was talking of going to the exhibition, so reluctantly agreed it was a chance of a lifetime, and with his 'sorry for himself look' even agreed to advance me a 'sub' of ten dollars.

So a little later, when school closed for a few days' holiday, officially Glenda travelled a hundred miles north to her parents' home. Whilst I happened to pick up the same time for my trip to Regina.

I was up early on a lovely summer's day; if the birds weren't singing, I thought they were, as I strode the fifteen miles into Lipton, four hours walking on air. There was no traffic, not that it was expected, for if anyone saw any motor transport on these minor dirt roads, in the course of a week it would create a conversation piece for weeks to come.

I caught a midday train into Regina, and later that day met Glenda at the exhibition. We *did* see over the exhibition, but most of the next day was spent basking in the sunshine in the wooded area around Wascana lake. Glenda stayed on with friends for a few days. Whilst I returned to Lipton the next day, and again, light-heartedly walked the fifteen miles back to Sam's.

That was a good summer for me: most evenings and spare time was spent at the Bartons with Glenda. And Sam was a good employer, inasmuch as life was easy going, and at least I could call Sam, "Sam", without it ever being suggested. Regardless of the fact that he was probably the oldest man I had worked for.

The crop looked reasonably good as harvest approached. The school closed for the long summer holiday, and Glenda returned home. As harvest began, I received a letter from Glenda, saying she would not be returning to that school, or the area, as expected in September, and in regretful words terminated our friendship.

Very soon the harvest was complete.

I don't know how many bushels of grain poor old Sam carted into town, just to cover the thirty-five dollars wages he owed me. The minute I had got the letter I had told him I would be leaving after harvest.

"I'll just try my luck somewhere else", I had said.

So one calm fall day, Sam took me into town, with another load of wheat, paid me the money he owed me, then unexpectedly said, "Let's have a meal." We sat rather uncomfortably over a good meal, I, feeling intimidated at knowing he was spending money he could ill afford. Then a handshake, a gruff, "All the best, Bill", and he was gone. 'Old Sam', who I would remember with a certain wistfulness.

And then on the train, through the parched brown prairie of 1933. Back to Regina. No welcome this time, the old boss, Mr. Surtees, was ill. Karl was working in the workshop on his own; there was very little business, an air of despondency. The next day I left my case and guitar with Karl and headed out of town, towards the north to look for work, anything to get away from the drought stricken plains.

I remember, as a hitchhiker, being dropped off at this little northern town called Spiritwood.

"I'll give you fifteen dollars a month."

I had been standing idly watching this blacksmith working. He was a middle-aged Indian, stripped to the waist, leather trousers and sandals, pouring with sweat, but what a physique: muscles bulging as he swung his hammer methodically on some metal he was working on, on the anvil. I had time on my hands, and so had been standing, staring at the blacksmith at work. After a while he stopped, put his hammer down and stood looking quizzically and unsmiling at me. Then without preamble he had said, "I'll give you fifteen dollars a month if you want work."

"What doing?", I queried.

"Can you drive a five horse outfit with disk?"

"Sure", I said.

"Right, I'll take you out to my farm, ten miles, when I'm finished here."

Why not, I thought, it's early fall, might as well earn a few dollars. It was late when he finished at the forge, and we drove in an old 'banger' to his farm.

At least the frame farmhouse was big enough, but as we entered, it was immediately noticeable that there were no floor coverings - bare boards, or curtains. Our footsteps made a distinctly hollow sound. He made a fire in the large grate in the kitchen, put a coffee pot on, pointed to various cupboards and said, "Help yourself to food".

Upstairs, a bare bedroom with a single bed and a few bed coverings. Nothing else, bare floorboards, blank uncovered windows.

Heck! So what. I slept soundly.

A voice aroused me. "Five o'clock". As I came to I was very conscious of two dull, but large expressionless brown eyes just above me, very close, as he repeated, "Five o'clock", then he was gone.

I dressed, went downstairs, and he pointed to the coffee pot percolating on the stove. I drank a quick cup, then we went and called the horses from the pasture, fed them in their stalls, then he watched as I harnessed them ready for disking. He pointed to a gate that led into the field I was to work.

We returned to the house, he pointed and said, "Help yourself to food, I'm going to town, be back this evening."

I worked in the field all morning. About midday I fed and watered the horses, made myself a meal, and worked all the afternoon. Again fed and watered the horses, and prepared another meal.

I had turned the horses out to pasture, when late in the evening he returned. It was a most peculiar set up, no women, nobody?

He walked over to where I had been disking all day, seemed satisfied; it was September, nearly dark, when he came back and said, "I'm off to bed", and was off upstairs without another word.

The second morning, "Five o'clock", aroused me, and there were those implacable dull staring eyes right above me, giving me the creeps. If only we could talk, but no, somehow there wasn't anything to say. The day proceeded as the previous one.

Late that evening I did pass an opinion, that the field I was working in was so infected with couch grass, it needed ploughing, not just disking. He just grunted.

The third morning, I shivered as I awoke to "Five o'clock", and those blasted lustreless eyes within inches of me. Why on earth was he so near, I woke easily, no need for closeness. His eyes were really worrying me now; if there had been a spark in them, a glimmer of warmth… It was the big dullness that now set my imagination on fire. He was gone, - "Call me Jim", he had said, and that was literally all I knew of him - when I returned from harnessing the horses.

I made myself some breakfast, and took stock. Quickly then deciding this wasn't for me. The Indian didn't owe me enough money for it to matter, anyhow money was not the thing worrying me at present. So I went out, unharnessed the horses, and drove them to pasture. Packed enough food to last the day, and with a last look round, slammed the door and was once again 'on my way', a free spirit, striding off in the opposite direction to Spiritwood. Soon putting miles behind me, till I would come to a main road or railway line.

And 'Old Queer Eyes' gradually fading into the past.

IV ~ Atlantic Time

Ottawa!

I had slept well, but was up early on that first morning. A bright sunny day, a few degrees below freezing, but comfortable.

I washed and shaved, taking my time, but then becoming impatient I put my coat and cap on, and went out into the little reception hall, where I handed my key over, thinking I might be quizzed over my changed appearance. But the little man still sitting behind his desk, as if he had been there all night, didn't even notice me. He obviously saw many strange faces; what was one more!

A little deflated, I walked along the street, bought a loaf of bread from a general store, and surreptitiously broke portions off, feeling somewhat self-conscious with so many people passing by. However, once again I was ravenously hungry, and that new baked bread was amazingly tasty. I ate half the loaf, and spread the remainder amongst my pockets for later.

As the morning advanced, and having made enquiries, I made my way to the government buildings and eventually located the Passport Office.

In the waiting room was a family of Indians, not indigenous North American Indians, whom one did see around occasionally, but two adults with two children from India, in traditional dress and headgear. The man was arguing, though somewhat obsequiously, with an official. But the official had an extremely haughty manner, and one sensed instantly that regardless of the rights or wrongs of their animated discussion, he considered himself far superior to anyone with a coloured skin. In fact he suddenly broke off the conversation and turned to me with a polite, "Can I help you, Sir?" I went towards him, and in a few words explained that I had a completed passport application form, signed and sealed in Regina. He said, "Come with me", and we entered another small office, where we sat, whilst he went through the form with me. Such a contrast, he couldn't have been more helpful or civil.

After a short conversation about where I was going, and particularly London, he simply said, "Come back at three thirty this afternoon and collect your passport." Passing out through the reception room where the now seated Indian family all smiled pleasantly at me, I left the building, though I had a feeling of unease.

Somehow, I had noticed before, officialdom in Canada often seemed more English than the English. Many men holding public office were English, and the old school tie attitude shone through. I had benefited by it, but wished I hadn't.

I remembered another incident, way back in 1931, when I was working on the Bruce farm. I had written to my parents at the time of the great dust storms, telling them of the depression, and the government schemes to keep men on the land. Dad had been very worried about me - I learnt many years later - and had written to his Member of Parliament about me, and conditions generally, in Canada.

Months later, unexpectedly, I received a letter from an immigration officer in Regina, suggesting if I liked to return to Regina they would find me another job, otherwise would I please reassure my parents that I was Ok. I never did anything about it, but was amazed that my descriptions of conditions of the time had reached so far, and had gone full circle back to me.

Hours now to kill. No money for food, the remains of my loaf must sustain me for the rest of the day.

Once, when I had first arrived in Regina, whilst talking to some youths of my own age, one had said, "Say, Buddy, what's that Buckingham Palace like?" Then for the first time in my life the realisation had hit me. That I had never seen it. I was born in North London, lived all my life, till

I was sixteen, in London, yet except for visits, very rarely, with the school to museums, I had never seen the famous sights of the biggest, most important capital city in the world.

I remember that youth staring at me incredulously. I had lived within ten or fifteen miles of all those historic places, and not seen them. Hard to believe!

So now I had a few hours to spare in the Canadian capital city. Okay, I'll find the legislative buildings, and when some day, someone asks what Ottawa was like, I'll have seen a little more than the freight yards.

The Parliament buildings are dignified, and *do* form the centre of the city, and although everywhere was covered in a layer of snow, the general appearance was massively and attractively Victorian. It was far from the best time of year to go sightseeing, but I was impressed. This capital was far superior to any prairie city.

However, without deliberately intending to, my eyes had been drawn like a magnet to the Ottawa River, north of the legislative buildings. I was worried: it looked suspiciously still, snow covered and frozen. The Ottawa River entered the St Lawrence River, one hundred and fifty miles east, quite near Montreal, and I was banking on arriving in Montreal before the river became unnavigable. For three or four months in the depths of winter, no ships could use the river, as the ice gradually thickened. So I tried to console myself by assuming that the St Lawrence, being one of the great rivers of the world, could not possibly have frozen yet. I wandered around as the hours dragged by. I was hungry, but I daren't spend any of my last few coins until I reached Montreal. The sights might be impressive, but I had too many things on my mind to appreciate them.

I was back at the passport office, dead on time, three thirty. My brand new passport was ready. The same official was most agreeable, wishing me a good journey and a happy Christmas. But again, I was made uneasy, by noting that the same Indian family were still sitting in the waiting room, impassively, but smiling as ever. Surely they hadn't been there all day. I will never know.

Now what to do? I am elated, I have my passport. But Montreal is still over a hundred miles away. It is late on a winter's afternoon, soon be dusk.

However, I think, if I walk to the eastern side of the city, and find the railroad tracks, any train going east must surely be going to Montreal. It is too late to attempt to hitch hike. It will be dark before I reach the city limits, and nobody gives lifts after dark.

So I walked towards the eastern outskirts. It was dark, but moonlight, by the time I found the east-west railway tracks, and was still in doubt, what to do?

The area was of small roads, and an odd house dotted here and there, fences, quite wooded, not the open and spacious tracks I was used to. I was feeling distinctly uncomfortable. No sound of trains in any direction. If I walked east along the line, away from the city, a train might be going too fast for me to jump, whereas if I walked towards the centre towards the rails I would be steadily approaching a more populous area. I decided to walk a little in the direction of the 'lights'.

Then it happened! Suddenly, unexpectedly, from seemingly nowhere, a big burly figure moved out of the shadows and accosted me. Long overcoat, fur hat and belted holster at the waist, a railway cop! A hand grabbed my arm, "Where do you think you're going?" I was so dumfounded I froze. Utter panic within. "Waiting for a friend", I replied. The sheer inadequacy of what I had said: the thought of meeting someone at a dark isolated spot, miles from anywhere, dimly struck me.

But then I was so unprepared for being accosted, I had no excuse ready, not that that really mattered at the moment.

Holding my arm he said, "Have you any money?"

"Not a cent", I responded, shaking like a leaf within, but now trying to appear indifferent.

He undid the buttons of my overcoat, and frisked me, starting at my armpits, down over my hips, and as his hand slid over my hundred dollar roll of notes my heart nearly stopped. But a miracle! He obviously hadn't related that lump in my pocket with money, and anyhow he would hardly expect a hobo wandering in the rail tracks to have any money.

Then he suddenly spun me around, and with an enormous kick up the backside sent me sprawling in the snow, at the same time saying, "If I catch you round here again I'll run you in as a vagrant."

I scrambled to my feet, and ran and ran. I just ran for ages, in a blind panic, down country roads. I didn't know where I was, sweating with fear. And yet as my pounding heart slowed down, a sense of elation began to take over. I slowed to a walk, 'such a close thing'.

If he had found the money he would have kept it, of that I was convinced. But, I still had it.

But what to do? I was stultified. Instinctively I was walking back towards the city centre. I had subconsciously already realised that I should not push my luck, when the goal was so close.

I still had some loose coins in my pocket. I dare not count them. I could get a bed for the night and hitch hike tomorrow. But that frozen river I had seen kept intruding into my thoughts and I still wanted to be 'on my way'.

A better idea occurred to me.

Not far from the centre, I found the railway station, and discovered there was a train leaving for Montreal just before midnight, a slow train, arriving early next morning. I counted my coins. Yes. A one dollar ticket to Montreal safely in my possession, a fresh loaf of bread divided amongst my pockets. Now I could while away many hours in the warm waiting room quite legitimately, and doze the night away in a real passenger train.

My mood had now changed so dramatically, since fully appreciating my lucky break, that although again shaking at the thought of it, I sat, covertly hoping that particular cop would appear and see me. And as I daydreamed I could see him on fire, screaming! Falling as a ball of fire from the sky, whilst I look on contemptuously.

But my memory slipped a long way back now…

I had triggered off a real nightmare. I was very young and frightened. Standing in my cot, clinging to the rails, and the terrific noise of anti-aircraft guns being fired. Dad had left his bed, reassuring us children. "There's nothing to worry about." He went to the window, partly pulled the curtains aside, and now! A blazing mass fills the sky, slowly falling, bright, brilliant orange, and small individual burning objects were falling also from the doomed Zeppelin. An imperishable memory. Then my mother's voice in the background, as I stood without understanding, but rigid with fear, "Close the curtains, Jack, it's horrible, horrible, that's men falling."

I was three years old. But many years later understood that there was great rejoicing over the Zeppelin that had been brought down at Cuffly, north of London.

I jerked out of my reverie as a railway cop did enter the waiting room and checked tickets. But I was now legitimate, and felt smug in my new and unaccustomed status. Anyhow, this wasn't the one, he was quite amenable, and I had no wish to see him burst into flames. How amiable he would have been to anyone without a ticket was questionable.

I had become an expert at dozing in comfortable or uncomfortable places, and soon slipped back, way back, in my dreams. Once again I am in a cot, but lying down very comfortably. I am watching the dappled sunlight shimmering through the window onto the wall, tree leaves moving with a gentle breeze, creating a kaleidoscope of patterns - my first conscious memory - warmth, fascinated by this picture. Then my mother's face, smiling, appeared above me, and another face beside her. Nan, this was my mother's friend, who, many years later we learnt, lived in a cottage in the New Forest. And although to my knowledge the friendship died with distance, an aura of mystery surrounded any talk of Mum's friend, Nan.

The New Forest itself lingered in my memory as some idyllic rendezvous with everlasting sunshine and tranquillity.

The stuff that dreams *are* made of.

Of this period I had one far more unpleasant recollection, but again vivid. I must have been two or three years old. In our small garden. Dad is on the opposite side of our tiny lawn and is calling, encouraging me, "Come on, Billy, you can do it. Keep trying, that's good, that's good", as I struggle to walk, with irons on my legs. Apparently I had rickets and had to learn to walk wearing these monstrosities, my arms outstretched towards Dad as I wobbled forwards.

***

Now, there is much activity, I come abruptly out of my daydreams. A train is in the station, its bell tolling rhythmically, the steam escaping with a loud hiss. They were giants, those Canadian Pacific locomotives; it didn't need much imagination to think of them as alive, a colossus rearing to go. I climbed aboard.

The train journey ended in Montreal, four or five hours hence. I was 'on my way', again!

So now I could sleep, and maybe dream, to the *clickety-clack, clickety-clack* of the wheels. For the first time since leaving Calgary, over two thousand miles, way back, I was paying my way. The forlorn wail of the train hooter signalled our departure.

Could I now really relax, put aside the thought of that frozen river? I had stood on the bank of the Ottawa River and fretted at the sight of that road of ice; it persisted in nagging at the back of my mind. Luck wouldn't thaw the ice, but had definitely been on my side with the railway cop.

Montreal in the morning. Then, I would know.

I snuggled in my seat in the half empty carriage, and again imagined - or did I - I heard the coyote's mournful howl echoing in the distance.

The train plodded through the night, a slow train, stopping and starting at numerous intermediate stations, the vague sound of voices as passengers boarded or alighted, keeping me now in a state of semi-sleep. And then the final slowing, slowing, as we juddered to a halt. Montreal! The Big City.

That imaginary distant howl of the coyote, very much a figment of my imagination. No wild animals around here.

Five o'clock in the morning, dark, cold, piles of snow everywhere. And where no attempt had been made to clear it, it was a foot deep and frozen solid.

131

Hopefully, no one would push me out of the waiting room, even the cops must sleep.

There was a scattering of people sitting around, and thankfully I was undisturbed. A few hours later, having bought a new loaf of bread and half eaten it, I made enquiries and located the Cunard shipping office; it was closed, but would open at ten o'clock. I wandered around killing time. Already I'd had many glimpses of the river, wide, solid, like a massive snow covered highway. No signs of boats or ships, making me feel despondent, as there was no pretence out there. And now, I really had to start thinking of how I could get to Halifax, another nine hundred miles away. Hitch hiking? Riding the freights?

Somehow, Montreal had been the destination, I hadn't thought beyond that; now I couldn't get the new possibility in focus. Maybe I was losing my nerve.

Montreal itself was so different to the prairie cities. As I wandered around, there was a compactness, similar in many ways to the Victorian parts of London: off the main street, narrow roads, and old substantial churches. An older, more mature appearance; these buildings were built to last and were here to stay. Not that I could take much interest in buildings, historical or otherwise, my mind was drawn insistently back to the river. I was at a low point of pessimism when I arrived back at the shipping office by ten o'clock. Well, the door was open! I would soon know my fate.

"Yes, Sir, what can I do for you?", asked the smartly dressed man behind the counter.

Take a deep breath...

"I want to book a passage to England, how much is it?"

"The cheapest fare is ninety-seven dollars, but the last liner sailed from here ten days ago, the next sailing is from Halifax, Nova Scotia, in three or four days' time."

I couldn't believe it. Halifax, that extra nine hundred miles. Although half expected, I was winded, defeated. I just stood there, empty and speechless.

132

The man across the counter said, "What's the problem?"

"I have only a hundred dollars, that's the problem", I said, fingering my still intact roll of notes.

"As I was saying", resumed the man across the counter, smiling somewhat sardonically, "it's ninety-seven dollars if the liner sails from here, but it's also ninety-seven dollars if the ship sails from Halifax. That includes train fare from here to Halifax, and train fare from Tilbury to St Pancras in London."

"The ticket is from Montreal to London, and you have three days from now to catch the *SS Ausonia*, due to arrive in Tilbury on 23rd of December. Do you still want to book?"

I pulled out my one hundred dollar roll of notes, and handed them over speechlessly, hardly believing it was happening. I was in a daze as he returned three one dollar bills, then handed me this long paper ticket with a, "Don't lose it, have a happy Christmas." I hesitated. "What do I do with my luggage?" "Book it into the train, label it *SS Ausonia* to London, and forget it till you disembark."

He grinned, "Going home?" I nodded in the affirmative and quickly left the office, far too full of emotion to speak.

Outside the sun was *not* shining, it was *not* warm, but I was inwardly glowing. I was exhilarated, I was trembling. I ate my last piece of bread. Three dollars left, and some small change. I immediately found a post office and spent one of my dollars on the briefest of cablegrams. *"Sailing SS Ausonia, Halifax, 16th December, Bill."* Knowing that Dad would check the 'ship arrivals' which were printed daily in the newspapers, and would be waiting for me on the boat train at St Pancras.

Everything was beginning to slip into place, as I returned to the station and checked train times. I had one more contemptuous look at that silent frozen river, I could cock a snook at it now, its threat was gone.

Eight o'clock the following morning the train was due to leave. Then, all day, all night, and another day the train would take on its journey to Halifax, arriving late in the day of the 15th. The following day, the 16th the liner would sail.

I found a cheap rooming house near the station and booked a room for forty cents. Then located the railway freight office - which was nowhere near the station - and claimed my old suitcase and crated guitar. In so doing giving me another peculiar feeling. Just seven days past, and well over two thousand miles back I was booking them into the freight offices in Calgary, wondering if I would ever collect them. I was still in a semi-daze, too much to take in.

I had to take a taxi to convey my guitar and case to my room, another forty cents. Now I could sit on my bed and try to relax and take stock of my position. Less than two dollars left, still more than three thousand miles from my destination, home. Forget it! I had a headache already; a weight had been lifted, but I still hadn't adjusted.

I now had to sort out my suitcase, and decide what to wear for the next seven days. Off my feet came my boots and overshoes, unlikely to need them again. A pair of brogues from the case, and maybe two pairs of socks. In the wash basin I rubbed out as best I could my underwear. Fortunately there were old fashioned radiators in the room, over which I could drape the few things washed. Then I had the luxury of a bath in the only bathroom along the corridor.

I repacked my case, even my faithful old blanket went in this time, and I was now wearing considerably less than during the past week.

I removed the slatted wooden crate from my guitar, strummed a few bars, put it back in its leather case, labelled it, along with my suitcase, and was all ready for departure, hours and hours ahead of time. I was trying desperately hard to keep myself busy; my headache persisted and I knew I was unlikely to sleep much that night. No point in going out into the freezing weather, I was hungry and completely disorientated. I walked up and down my tiny room, and later eventually lay down and dozed fitfully through the night.

At six o'clock I was up and washed, by seven I could get moving.

134

The wooden crate, my faithful old boots and overshoes, and many other items I knew I would never need again were left in a corner of the room.

I carried my case and guitar down to the small reception area. A man was sitting drowsily in a chair behind a desk. I placed my key on the counter and said, "I'm off now", and once again, out into the cold and snow.

The station was within walking distance, and in a short ten minutes I was there, booked my case and guitar right through. To be collected in London.

Once again I was almost light-headed with reaction. I no longer had that comforting roll of notes nestling in my pocket. Only a razor and a toothbrush, for through force of habit I still felt the need to have my hands free. But, I did have a passport and a through ticket to London.

I bought another, the inevitable loaf of bread, ten cents. Hot! I could have wolfed it down right off. But I distributed three quarters of it in paper bags in the various pockets of my overcoat which I was still wearing, ate the other quarter, and still had about an hour to wait for the train.

Still in a trance-like state when the train at last pulled in, bell ringing importantly, I boarded as if I had been riding passenger trains for the last five years.

A half empty train, luxuriously warm and spacious. I picked a window seat, prepared to read and idle the hours away. This time tomorrow we would still be plodding through New Brunswick and on into Nova Scotia later in the day. So time was likely to drag.

For the first few hours, travelling through the valley of the St Lawrence river, it was varied and attractive scenery, though as throughout my journey, everything was snow covered, which had a tendency to make everywhere look the same. I amused myself by following on my large map the riverside towns and villages we were passing through. And every once in a while surreptitiously eating some of my tucked away bread.

Around midday, many passengers had wandered off down the train to the dining car. I, had only got as far as the end of the carriage where there were toilets, and, as importantly, a drinking water tap.

There was a family of four, parents and two small children, sitting on the opposite side of the train, directly opposite to me. The youngsters were noisy and animated, but they were in the background, and I hadn't taken any real notice of them. Maybe I was more conspicuous than I was aware of, for out of the blue, a little girl of about eight years of age, broke into my reverie and said, "Mister, mummy said would you like some sandwiches? Mummy says we've got too many", at the same time offering me a paper plate with half a dozen sandwiches.

I could hardly stop drooling!

"Thank you, dear, tell your mummy thank you very much."

The taste of those ham sandwiches, which they turned out to be, lingered in my memory for ages. Bread may be the staff of life, especially when one is permanently hungry, but after seven days of little else, it had certainly lost its charm.

By late afternoon the passing terrain had become a monotonous flat farming country. Small holdings, deeply snow covered. But many irregular fields, even some hedges. This was old Canada, before the gridiron appearance of most of modern Canada took over. In summer, no doubt, it would be scenically very attractive, but now, in mid-winter it was bleak and uninteresting.

Shortly after it grew dark, the little girl's mother came across and sat down. Introducing herself as Mrs. Macdonald, and offering the information that she and her family were going to Halifax for Christmas, her parents' home, and that their Scottish forebears had settled there over a hundred years before.

By the time I had explained where I came from and where I was going - though a false kind of pride prevented me telling how I had arrived so far - the two little girls had wandered over, then the husband, who was rather more reserved. So now I had an interested audience; my cockney accent fascinated them, and I could ramble on, drifting over the years. The little girls interspersing every so often with, "Don't you talk funny."

The 'West' was as foreign to them as Europe. So my farming experiences were as strange to them as life in cockney London, which I was quite willing to talk about.

They lived in Quebec, and had travelled back and forth to Halifax, but that was their limit. They were settled, with roots well dug in, and although they obviously enjoyed listening about travel, they had no inclination to move about themselves.

Then of course the girls started saying they were hungry, "We want some supper". They soon rose to go to the dining car, suggesting I join them. I demurred, saying I wasn't hungry and would be eating later.

My stomach called me a liar, but only I heard.

The miles were still racing by, so I could once again slip into a reverie, and try to kid myself that hunger was not important, merely a state of mind, and if I didn't think about it, it would go away.

I was disturbed from my musings by the return of the family; as they passed towards their seats, Mrs. Macdonald plumped a package of sandwiches and a paper mug of coffee in front of me, saying, "Keep you going", and was gone. Again my emotions were stretched. I couldn't have thanked her even if she had given me the opportunity. For all my light-hearted chatting, they had obviously realised my predicament, and had done just the right thing, trying not to embarrass me.

It was late evening, everywhere people were folding the tables under the windows, pulling the seats together to make beds. As the train was less than half full, very few of the overhead locker bunks were used. I had four seats to convert to one double bed, a couple of blankets and a pillow from the locker. What more could I need, even my demanding stomach had ceased complaining.

I removed my shoes and jacket, and now, except for a faint yellow bulb at each end of the compartment, the lights were turned off as passengers composed themselves to sleep through the night.

I could stretch out now in warmth and comfort and doze off to the *clickety click, clickety click* of the wheels, and the distant, occasional, *oo-oo-ee*, that mournful evocative sound, always reminding me of the wilderness.

That melancholic expression of vast space would captivate my dreams long into the future, reminding me particularly of the virgin prairie and my first experience of farming. Picking rocks and listening, listening for that forlorn sound wafting fifteen miles across the plains.

***

But now, as I drifted into sleep, the *clickety click, clickety click* of the wheels became a *clap, clap, clap*, as my subconscious wandered back seven years to my last term at school. A prize giving was held every year just before Christmas. And *I* was walking down the centre of the assembly hall, like walking down an aisle, which was packed with children and their parents. All vigorously clapping me. *Me!* Who had just won the most prestigious prize of the school year: "The Gabling Cup for special progress". I was walking on air, and there at the side of the hall was Mr. Prince, clapping!

Mr. Prince was a teacher, a middle-aged, short, rotund man. He was our geography teacher, and I liked and shone at this subject. He generally carried a short thick cane, and did use it occasionally. But he had an authority that belied his shortness, so had no real need to use it; it's just that he was different in that respect, inasmuch as all the other teachers had long swishy canes which they all used as circumstances demanded. I liked Mr. Prince, he was sharp, he sparkled, and nobody was inattentive during his session. Admittedly I was his 'blue eyed boy', as I had come top, two years running in geography.

The headmaster, in his end of term speech - which would normally be something boring - had mentioned my name three times; at least, Dad said so, who was sitting proudly by my side. Mum was always far too self-conscious to attend any such ceremony.

In almost a trance I was presented with this large cup, plus a gold plated pocket watch. The cup would adorn our chiffonier in the parlour for six months, with my name engraved on it, above six present names.

'The Parlour', was of course, sacrosanct. Used only on special days,

138

the linoleum floor highly polished, everything spotless and in its place, and if we were allowed occasionally to play records on the new wind-up gramophone Dad had bought, Mum would be forever poking her nose in, to see we weren't disturbing anything.

I knew I was in line for the honour of winning this prize. I had come top of the class in various subjects the previous year, collecting a couple of prizes, and for two years had climbed steadily up the placings, from an 'average' to top of the class - of sixty - and this was the culmination. I swelled with pride on leaving the school; all eyes were on me, as with Dad I carried the cup home.

I was thirteen.

Six months later, when I would be leaving school on my fourteenth birthday, I would return the cup, where it would sit, the largest cup in a centrally placed glass cabinet in the assembly hall, for the rest of the year, and await its next proud owner.

***

Throughout the night the train rolled on. Every once in a while, through the obscurity of half sleep, one would realise the bell was ringing, and that we had stopped at some unknown town. Distant voices, people getting on and off, vague sounds of activity, but sleep quickly reasserted itself, until dawn broke greyly outside.

As soon as it was sufficiently light I was up. This was the penultimate day. Tomorrow I would be leaving Canada, a peculiar, almost sad emotion. Calgary seemed so far away, in time and in distance, ten days back, freezing on the first night of my train journey. And now, sometime during the night we had passed into the last time zone. Out of eastern time into Atlantic time. Four hours, and nearly three thousand miles from where I started. Was it only ten days ago? Heck!, but it did not really register.

I washed and shaved, drank some water and finished the last chunk of bread in my pocket.

Soon Mrs. Mac and family passed by, with a cheery "Good morning", this time, tactfully not asking me to join them for breakfast.

I sat watching the world go dreamily by, still the everlasting snow covered landscape; it seemed there was nowhere in Canada free of snow. 'White' did not predominate, it was absolute.

There were many small houses, chimneys smoking comfortably, smaller fields, a taste of old England, or more to the point old Scotland, as by midday we would be entering Nova Scotia, the 'New Scotland' of two centuries back, to arrive in Halifax by late afternoon.

The MacDonald family came trooping back. Mrs. Mac almost aggressively planting a packet of sandwiches and a paper mug of coffee in front of me, and a "Come and have a talk later", offer.

Coffee and ham sandwiches, 'nectar from heaven!'

I normally had a very big appetite, but for ten days my stomach had been sadly neglected. However my goal was only twenty-four hours away. *SS Ausonia* would supply me with three meals a day. I was, at last, beginning to believe I would make it.

I went over and chatted for an hour with the Mac family, and as it drew nearer to lunch time, I made my excuses and said I was going to spend some time at the rear of the train, in the observation car. The caboose at the end of the train had open verandas, very popular in the summer, but not at this time of year. I did not spend much time outside, it was cold and grey. I had begun to feel rather uncomfortable about the Mac's largesse, so I stayed at the back of the train to avoid a repetition. Only returning to my seat later as we drew into Truro, I unrolled my large map for the last time and checked that we were less than one hundred miles from our destination. It was getting dusk as we arrived late in the afternoon.

Halifax! The end of the line.

I had said my goodbyes, and thanks, to the Mac family, wishing and being wished a Happy Christmas.

Now a different, and to me, unknown city.

Halifax was founded by English settlers back in 1750, and named after an English earl. It was certainly one of the earliest colonies and one of the oldest parts of Canada. This semi-industrialised area had been, and was, suffering as much as the prairies from The Great Depression. But, being seemingly at the extreme eastern edge of Canada, the moving population of transients or hobos seldom rode the freights to this pocket or cul-de-sac. People hit by failure or unemployment stayed 'put', similar to the old country. Whereas the great army of unemployed drifted back and forth over the great open spaces of the plains, whether in Canada or the States. Though as one Canadian farmer expressed it, many years later, overnight they seemed to disappear, *when war was declared.*

But now I must find my ship. It was dark and damp cold. There was slushy snow everywhere, dirty, and a slightly foggy atmosphere. I was reminded immediately of England; the temperature hovered around freezing, houses were festooned with icicles where there was continuous freezing and thawing; there was no doubt we were beside the sea.

After making enquiries I made my way to the harbour; there were scattered lights, and in no time, there she was '*The SS Ausonia*', towering above the dockside like a colossus, belittling all the other craft around her, adorned with a mass of ice and frozen snow.

But, what an incredible sensation, impossible to express, as I read, and reread the large lettered name on the bow. Standing there, transfixed, open mouthed in awe, almost shivering with reaction. 'Snap out of it, Billy boy, you've made it'. Maybe I can get aboard.

There was a gangplank, across to a door in the side of the ship, but the door was firmly locked, and nobody about. I eventually found the offices of the harbour master, and explained my predicament to an official - that I had no money, that I would be sailing tomorrow on the *Ausonia*, and was it possible to board today. But although he was sympathetic, as expected, he told me that no passengers were allowed to board before ten o'clock the next day. And that the liner would be sailing, on the tide, at three o'clock in the afternoon.

So I had a long night to kill.

I wasn't tired, I couldn't have slept even if I'd had a bed; I was restless and agitated as I wandered around the empty streets. I did discover 'Province House', the colonnaded parliament buildings; after all, I was in the capital city of the province of Nova Scotia, but I couldn't work up any enthusiasm as a sightseer. Apart from it being dark and cold and snow-covered, my feet were irresistibly drawn back to the harbour, and the lofty presence of the liner. A little later I made my way back to the railway station, where with some of my last few coins, I sat over a cup of coffee in the station buffet.

I still had that one dollar bill in my pocket, which for some unexplainable reason I must keep, like an insurance, though what use it could be in a real emergency I couldn't imagine.

The station closed at midnight, and the buffet with it. Now I only had ten hours to kill in a completely deserted, sleeping city. I would walk about and keep warm, have an other look at '*Ausie*', and generally kill time. Needless to say the sheer emptiness of the streets made the time drag. But not unexpectedly, during the early hours, a local policeman hove into sight, patrolling his lonely beat.

With my ticket and passport in my pocket I was quite at ease, no cop could worry me now, or deflate me. I was still floating on air. He did accost me, in the friendliest way. I explained my intention of sailing later that day, we chatted, and he turned up trumps, by suggesting, that if I liked to be at the police station in an hour's time, he would be there, and I could stay with him in the waiting room, "till his shift finished at seven in the morning". Gratefully I accepted his offer.

This policeman was another example of someone born and bred in Halifax, who had never travelled more than a hundred miles from home, and yet was fascinated by the tales of travellers. But the coffee he supplied was the greatest gift of all, as we sat and chatted until seven o'clock in the morning.

By eight o'clock I was wandering up and down the harbour side, past 'my' ship, and back again. By nine o'clock, other would-be passengers began to gather. Until by ten o'clock - when the door at the end of the gangway was opened - about fifty people were ready to board.

I was one of the first aboard. Passport and customs formalities were quickly dealt with, and now I could set about finding my cabin. The *SS Ausonia*, a Cunard liner of seventeen thousand tons, to me, was gigantic. Passages, staircases and doors everywhere. At last I found my cabin. Four berths, two bunks on each side, one above the other, a let-down wash basin, standing or laying room only. Heck! So what! I was far too elated to consider such trifles. I left my overcoat lying on my bunk, to show that someone was already in occupation, and found my way to the deck.

I watched as a steady stream of passengers boarded the ship. The appearance of the ship from where I was standing was most unattractive: everywhere was slushy trodden down snow, there were so many dripping icicles it was like an arctic spring, and, although for the first time on my journey the temperature was hovering above freezing, a general atmosphere of neglect seemed to rule.

However, first lunch was to be served at noon, and I was there on the dot. To have a 'steward', all dressed up to kill, offer me a menu - I didn't believe it. I have a choice? That first three course meal will be remembered for a long time. *Boy!* I had missed my meals.

Replete, I could now join most of the other passengers on deck, as preparations were made for departure. Only a few stragglers were boarding now, as a couple of fat little tugs were fussily arranging themselves to pull us away from the dockside. Suddenly, with a clatter, the gangway is pulled aboard. A pause, then a mighty roar from the ship's siren, denoting imminent departure, as the powerful tugs inch us away from the harbour wall. What an incredible moment of nostalgia, and how monstrously huge the liner appears, as she is towed slowly by the tugs to the harbour entrance.

Everything appears to happen in slow motion, as shortly we are at sea. Our escorts have tooted and gone, the ship's own powerful engines

143

throbbing and driving us steadily eastwards. In the dusk and distance the Canadian shoreline fast fading away, and yet again '*I am on my way*'.

'Our Lady of the Snows', Kipling called Canada, and surely anyone travelling across Canada in winter could not dispute that term. For my three thousand mile journey the landscape was completely white, snow covered. Only in Halifax, the all season gateway, or back door of Canada did one notice a difference, where the ocean predominated.

And now as the decks slowly emptied, I lingered awhile, trying to understand and absorb the apparent infinity of the ocean, which like the prairies, had fascinated me by this vastness. It was all sea and sky now in every direction, and would remain so for seven days as the liner, now only a speck in that immensity, forged relentlessly across the mighty Atlantic.

I eventually went below, and met my cabin companions. Two Danes and a Scotsman. The Danes, who were middle-aged were returning home, having sold up their farm, completely disillusioned, and had no idea what the future held for them. They were victims of a depression that had already lasted five years, and seemed endless and beyond comprehension. The Scotsman, older than me, was also returning home.

There was a complete transformation the following morning; the crew had been busy, the temperature had risen, and *at last*, not a sign of snow or ice anywhere. The ship was spick and span, though the sky was grey and heavy with the promise of rain. We would glimpse the sun rarely during the next seven days, mostly the damp dull weather would persist throughout the voyage.

There was, I felt, a subtle difference in comparing the passengers on this voyage, to those emigrating to Canada on my outward journey. Admittedly, generally they were older, but they were also quieter, and certainly lacked the animation one had felt, expressed by those 'Going West'. Maybe it was purely personal, as I still felt a lot younger than those around me.

I was twenty-one, and my twenty-first birthday still stood out vividly.

***

Only a few months previously I had been working on the 'Regina City Farm', one of six hired men. This farm on the outskirts of Regina, and provincially owned, encompassed a farm, a public park, and a golf course; and the six of us had varying jobs to do apart from normal farm work. The golf course was eighteen hole, standard size, but the greens were not grass. No doubt because of drought conditions, grass could not be kept growing, so the 'greens' were filled with oiled sand, which acted very well, the balls rolling smoothly over the surface, but when used often, one of us would be spending a day raking and rolling the 'greens' to keep them flat, in between the golfers using the course. I had been hired as a 'horse man', and mostly I was driving a horse outfit on general farm work.

We lived in a bunk house, whilst the manager and his wife lived in a house nearby. Three times a day we all adjourned to 'the house', and sat round a large dining table, eight of us, and had our meal. We ate quickly and silently, three good large meals a day, but there was no pleasure in it. Why nobody was ever able to create conversation I never understood. Maybe it was the manager and his wife, who were both so taciturn never seeming to encourage it. He was the least talkative of the non-talkers.

But amongst the six of us there was plenty of bantering and fun. My birthday fell on a Saturday in mid-July.

George, who was the eldest of us, about forty, and always had bright ideas said, "On Saturday, let's all go to the fair, and celebrate Bill's birthday with a flagon of wine." All agreed, and so on a lovely hot Saturday afternoon we trooped into town, firstly purchasing a gallon flagon of wine; blueberry wine if I remember right, and proceeded to the fair, swigging the wine as we felt inclined. It was heavy, so we needed to reduce the weight, and it was hot, so maybe it would also reduce our thirst?

A circus had come to town, and we enjoyed the sideshows and various amusements. After an hour, Joey, the youngest of us - he was eighteen - slid to the ground, sozzled! We were all a bit worse for wear, but we dragged him into a cul-de-sac, removed his wallet and wristwatch and continued enjoying ourselves. The flagon was quite light by now. I don't remember much more.

It would seem that I was loudly singing 'Home on the Range', when

George got a taxi, and shepherded us all back to the farm. I do remember being violently sick that night, and not wanting to talk to anybody next day, especially about my twenty-first birthday.

***

Our ship soon settled into a set routine. Three very good meals a day, though there were many empty tables as the liner was far from full. Many passengers walked the decks endlessly round and round, determined to keep fit, whilst above all I enjoyed the large lounge and games room. I was enthralled by the newly popular game of auction bridge, soon found a foursome, and played for hours. This was interspersed by chess or darts, so one could spend practically the whole day playing games. By the second day four of us had emerged as keen chess players, fairly equal in ability.

It was a day later when I made such an arrogant blunder. Whilst engrossed in a game, I became aware of someone standing watching. Looking up I recognised one of my cabin companions, one of the Danish brothers. He said, "Maybe you would give me a game later?" "Sure", I replied.

So a little later we sat down to play. He had said he hadn't played much. Playing carefully - with an unknown - I beat him. He asked, "Shall we have another?", "Ok", I said. Then sensing his lack of experience, I made the one, two, three moves, without any relevant defensive moves coming from him. Then the fourth, "Checkmate", I said. He sat looking, not really understanding, not really believing. I felt terrible, what a *faux pas*. "Sorry", I apologised, "Scholar's Mate, thought you would know". He was still staring quietly at the board and said, "I had no idea".

If he had been a man of my own age, I don't think it would have bothered me, but he was a polite, nice man, old enough to be my father. And I wished, so much, that I hadn't tried to be clever. Thankfully, for the remainder of the voyage he was as friendly as ever, no animosity, though he never suggested another game.

146

Each day the large clock in the dining room was reset by about forty minutes, as the liner forged eastwards so we were gaining time each day, and the distance in miles travelled the previous day was set in large figures above the clock.

Early on the sixth day, everybody is beginning to get excited. Crowds on deck, expectantly, more chatter now, but all eyes looking ahead. And then, somebody with sharp eyes calls, "Land in sight". Soon we can all make out that dark smudge, the isles of Scilly, gradually appearing on the horizon.

Now, everybody is on deck, as slowly the true mainland coastline becomes visible. Cliffs, grey and white, majestic! Soon, what hardly anyone can believe, *green* grass. It seems no longer winter. The excitement, the enthusiasm was all of the green freshness, as all day we steamed up the English Channel, savouring the colour, decks crowded, everyone voicing their appreciation.

Next morning when we awoke early, we found we were well up the Thames. Industrial activity predominating, the river banks quite close now. Chimneys belching smoke, grey skies, and that lovely green freshness of yesterday, gone.

But the thrill - there was a vibrancy in the air - was still persisting. Everybody was on deck again. The excitement was contagious, as by midmorning the little tugs attached themselves to our liner, and pulled and pushed and shoved her into this seemingly tiny pool of a harbour. They knew their job, and at last the big ship was at rest; now the sound of the strength of the huge throbbing engines could subside, becoming only a murmur.

I felt like patting old 'Ausie' on the back - sorry, deck - and saying, "Good old girl, take a rest." Now everybody deserted the decks to get to the disembarkation points, and on to their various destinations. Having said goodbye to my many travelling friends I proceeded in a queue through passport and customs formalities, and then down the gangplank to the harbour side. Having collected my suitcase and guitar, I could now pause and take stock. I felt strange, it didn't feel like 'home'; everything was too compact, too close, a sense of claustrophobia.

Though what was 'home' meant to feel like…?

There was the boat train for St Pancras, a silly little train, hissing gently. I boarded with the rest of the passengers, still being unable to take in the smallness and congestion of everything around me. Little engines with short carriages, and compartments made to take ten or a dozen people, sitting in two rows, facing each other, knees nearly touching. Heck! Give me space!

Then that pathetic shrill whistle, and we were off, out of the station still milling with people, and immediately passing through valleys of small brick houses, with hundreds of smoking chimneys, little fenced gardens, all packed together in narrow roads. And maybe for the first time, the vastness and openness of Canada was really brought home to me.

'St Pancras'. Moment of truth.

I still had my one solitary, unspendable dollar bill in my pocket. No use in England.

I alighted, a sigh of relief. There, up on the platform, amongst the crowds, was my unmistakable, jaunty, Dad. Jumping, grinning and waving. Though who the glamour girl standing beside him was, just didn't register. My sister, Nancy, was just fourteen when I left home, now nineteen, an impossible transformation.

A handshake, a kiss, mixed feelings.

We caught a bus for our home in North London. Conversation was stilted, difficult. We were like strangers, feeling their way with each other. It would be many hours before we were completely relaxed.

A small brick house, tiny front garden with the inevitable privet hedge.

We had arrived.

My two kid brothers, Jeff now fourteen, and Vic now eleven, with my elder brother Arthur in the background. All open mouthed and self-conscious at the door. But my mother, pushing forward, my retiring, undemonstrative mother, just grabbed my arms with both hands, her eyes glistening - *"BILL!"*

And I was home.